# Contents

GW01218314

| | | |
|---|---|---:|
| | The material for years 3, 4 and 5 of SMP 11–16 | 2 |
| | Introduction to *Book R2* | 4 |
| | Notes and answers for *Book R2* | 5 |
| 1 | Using a calculator | 5 |
| 2 | In your head (1) | 6 |
| 3 | Averages | 6 |
| 4 | Equations and formulas (1) | 8 |
| 5 | Angles | 9 |
| 6 | Proportionality (1) | 10 |
| 7 | Equations and formulas (2) | 11 |
| 8 | Gradient | 12 |
| | Review 1 | 13 |
| 9 | In your head (2) | 14 |
| 10 | Equations and formulas (3) | 15 |
| 11 | Area | 16 |
| 12 | Proportionality (2) | 17 |
| 13 | On paper (1) | 21 |
| 14 | Plans and elevations | 22 |
| 15 | Rates | 23 |
| | Review 2 | 24 |
| 16 | Simplifying expressions | 25 |
| 17 | In your head (3) | 26 |
| 18 | Contours | 27 |
| 19 | Brackets | 27 |
| 20 | Probability | 28 |
| 21 | The circle | 30 |
| 22 | On paper (2) | 31 |
| 23 | Sampling | 31 |
| | Review 3 | 47 |

# The material for years 3, 4 and 5 of SMP 11–16

The yellow, blue, red and green series together make up the second part of the SMP 11–16 course, for pupils in the third to fifth years of secondary school (ages 13+ to 16+).

(The booklet scheme which forms the first part of the course is fully described in the *Teacher's guides* for levels 1, 2, 3 and 4, and the *Practical guide*.)

The overall structure of the material for years 3 to 5 is set out in the diagram below.

The Y series is for the most able group of pupils (roughly speaking, the top 20% to 25% or so, although the proportion is likely to vary from school to school). The B and R series are for the 'middle' group (the next 35% to 40% or so) and the G series for lower ability pupils (apart from those with special learning difficulties).

The B series branches after *Book B2* to allow the more able of the pupils in the middle group to move ahead on to more demanding work in the R series. The mathematical content of the R series has much in common with that of *Books Y1, Y2* and *Y3*, but presentation and pace are often different.

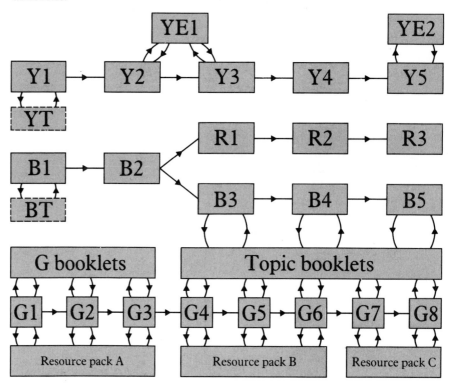

The two YE books are 'extension' books written to stretch the most able pupils. *Books YT* and *BT* are transition books written for pupils who have not previously followed the booklet scheme in years 1 and 2.

## Classroom organisation and teaching style

It is assumed that pupils will be grouped in sets according to ability in the third, fourth and fifth years.

Although there is rather more exposition and explanation in the books than is found in many other textbooks, the books are not intended to be 'self-instructional'. Many important points arise in the course of doing the problems in the books, and these points will need to be brought out by the teacher in discussion with the whole class or with smaller groups or as appropriate. Teachers may find it possible from time to time to give particular chapters or sections of chapters to the class to work through on their own, which is no bad thing since the ability to pick up information from the printed page and to follow written explanations is an important one. Where this is done it will be necessary for the teacher carefully to 'go over' what has been done.

There are no 'chapter summaries'. The writers feel it is more valuable for classes to make their own summary notes. The ideal ultimately is for each pupil to make his or her own notes, but initially it may be better for the teacher to lead a discussion after each chapter of the main ideas before any notes are made.

# Introduction to Book R2

*Mental and written arithmetic and the use of calculators*

It is assumed throughout that unless there is an instruction to the contrary calculators will be used for all but the simplest calculations which can be done mentally.

We strongly recommend that teachers encourage mental calculation, and from time to time give short sets of questions to be answered mentally. We also suggest having occasional practice sessions on written arithmetic, but that the scope of these should not extend beyond addition, subtraction, multiplication by 2, 3, . . . 9 and division by 2, 3, . . . 9 of whole numbers and money.

*Starred sections and questions*

Occasional sections and questions are starred to indicate that they are of greater difficulty and can be left out by slower pupils using the book.

*Equipment needed*

Certain standard items of equipment are needed frequently and no special attention is drawn to them in the books. These include rulers, angle measurers (recommended for angle measurement; see below), compasses, scissors and 2 mm graph paper.

In other cases, equipment needed (such as tracing paper) is referred to in the book. Worksheets are needed occasionally. Masters for these are available separately (see below). Five worksheets are needed for the *Book R2*, numbered R2–1 to R2–5.

Pupils working from the R series are assumed to have the use of a scientific calculator.

*Ordering equipment*

The following items required for *Book R2* are published by Cambridge University Press. You should order them through your usual school book supplier.

Worksheet masters for *Books B4*, *R2* and *Y4*    ISBN 0 521 32586 2
Angle measurers (pack of 5)    ISBN 0 521 25435 3
Database cards (pack of 10)    ISBN 0 521 33182 X

When ordering, remember to state the ISBN, the series title (SMP 11–16), the name of the item, the publisher and the number of **packs** you want. (So, for example, if you want 35 angle measurers, write your order as '7 packs of 5'.)

# Notes and answers for Book R2

## 1  Using a calculator

This chapter is concerned with calculations involving more than one operation, e.g. $872 - (26 \times 18)$. Calculators handle the order of operations in different ways, hence the distinction made in the chapter between the two main types of calculator.

### A  Order of operations

**A1**  Pupil's check on type of calculator

**A2**  LTR 8,  MDF 5

**A3**

|  | LTR | MDF |
|---|---|---|
| (a) | 130 | 18 |
| (b) | 2 | 7 |
| (c) | ⁻1 | 8 |
| (d) | 33 | 6 |
| (e) | 5 | 7 |
| (f) | 1 | 7 |

### B  Calculations with brackets (1)

**B1**  (a) 20  (b) 24  (c) 5
(d) 20  (e) 4  (f) 16

**B2**  (a) 24·6  (b) 42·9  (c) 22·6
(d) 21·84  (e) 6  (f) 6·75

### C  Calculations with brackets (2)

**C1**  (a) 22·55  (b) 17·75  (c) 23·6
(d) 17·2  (e) ⁻0·4  (f) 2

**C2**  (a) 4  (b) 7  (c) 4  (d) 3

**C3**  (a) 6  (b) 48  (c) 268
(d) 25 172  (e) 3045  (f) ⁻11

**C4**  (a) 14·2  (b) 0·3  (c) 79·1
(d) 3·2  (e) ⁻17·4  (f) 52·5
(all to 1 d.p.)

### D  Substituting into formulas

Discussion may be needed in this section regarding the appropriate degree of accuracy in the final answers.

**D1**  (a) 8  (b) 18
(both to the nearest whole number)

**D2**  (a) 178·56  (b) 179·2  (c) 179·76

**D3**  (a) 366  (b) 125
(both to the nearest whole number)

**D4**  (a) 1746  (b) 780
(both to the nearest whole number)

**D5**  (a) 122  (b) 246
(both to the nearest whole number)

# 2 In your head (1)

This chapter is about mental addition and subtraction of two-digit numbers. Different people have different methods of doing mental arithmetic and a discussion of the various methods used by the class can be valuable. The methods suggested in the chapter are not of course intended to be imposed on pupils who have adequate methods of their own!

## Adding and subtracting

1  (a) 14  (b) 22  (c) 31  (d) 53  (e) 44
   (f) 9   (g) 18  (h) 76  (i) 35  (j) 59

2  (a) 59  (b) 61  (c) 33  (d) 58  (e) 47
   (f) 92  (g) 98  (h) 73  (i) 77  (j) 39

3  (a) 59  (b) 72  (c) 91  (d) 83  (e) 52
   (f) 78  (g) 74  (h) 82  (i) 54  (j) 82

4  £39. Pupils are asked to explain their methods here. Various different explanations are acceptable.

5  (a) 18  (b) 33  (c) 44  (d) 49  (e) 38
   (f) 48  (g) 45  (h) 36  (i) 54

6  (a) 16  (b) 51  (c) 14  (d) 7   (e) 15
   (f) 16  (g) 58  (h) 58  (i) 37  (j) 69

7  (a) 73p  (b) 28 minutes  (c) 64 lb
   (d) 49p  (e) 35 minutes  (f) 67p
   (g) 29 miles  (h) £1·05

# 3 Averages

This chapter introduces the mean, including the mean of a frequency distribution. Section E looks at some examples of situations where the mean can be a misleading average to use and where the median may be better.

## A  The median: a review

A1  £95,  £108, £114, £116, £120, £125, £132, £144, £153, £155, £160, £172, £188
    Median £132

A2  43, 48, 48, 52, 59, 63, 63, 65, 67, 74, 78, 85, 90, 92
    Middle pair 63, 65;   median 64

## B  The mean

B1  97·0 kg

B2  55·8 kg

B3  282 miles

B4  Pupil's measurements may vary by at least 0·1 cm from those given here but still be acceptable.

| Measured lengths in cm | 4·8 | 9·0 | 5·5 | 7·2 | 3·8 | 8·3 |
|---|---|---|---|---|---|---|
| Real lengths in cm | 24·0 | 45·0 | 27·5 | 36·0 | 19·0 | 41·5 |

Mean length 32·2 cm (to 1 d.p.)

**B5**  17·7 °C (to 3 s.f)

**B6**  (a)  Jane 13·3,  Neeta 13·1   (b)  Jane

**B7**  (a)  1·56 miles   (b)  1·68 miles
       (both to 2 d.p.)

## C  Calculating the mean from frequencies

**C1**  (a)

| Weight | Frequency | Weight of group |
|--------|-----------|-----------------|
| 2 g    | 7         | 14 g            |
| 3 g    | 10        | 30 g            |
| 4 g    | 12        | 48 g            |
| 5 g    | 4         | 20 g            |
| Total  | 33        | 112 g           |

(b)  Mean weight 3·4 g

**C2**  (a)

| Number of matches in box | Frequency (number of boxes) | Number of matches in group |
|--------------------------|-----------------------------|----------------------------|
| 46 | 8  | 368  |
| 47 | 19 | 893  |
| 48 | 46 | 2208 |
| 49 | 15 | 735  |
| 50 | 12 | 600  |
| Total | 100 | 4804 |

(b)  Mean 48·0

**C3**  2·3 people

## D  Grouped data

**D1**  (a)  27·5 kg

(b)

| Weight in kg | Mid-interval value | Number of boys | Weight of group |
|--------------|--------------------|----------------|-----------------|
| 20–25 | 22·5 | 10 | 225  |
| 25–30 | 27·5 | 40 | 1100 |
| 30–35 | 32·5 | 60 | 1950 |
| 35–40 | 37·5 | 50 | 1875 |
| 40–45 | 42·5 | 20 | 850  |
| Total |      | 180 | 6000 |

(c)  Mean weight 33 kg (to nearest kg)

**D2**  (a)

| Weight in kg | Mid-interval value | Number of girls | Weight of group |
|--------------|--------------------|-----------------|-----------------|
| 25–30 | 27·5 | 20 | 550  |
| 30–35 | 32·5 | 50 | 1625 |
| 35–40 | 37·5 | 60 | 2250 |
| 40–45 | 42·5 | 40 | 1700 |
| Total |      | 170 | 6125 |

(b)  Mean weight 36 kg (to the nearest kg)
(c)  The girls are heavier than the boys, on average.

**D3**  (a)

| Length of call in s | Mid-interval value | Number of calls | Total length in group |
|---------------------|--------------------|-----------------|-----------------------|
| 0–40    | 20  | 5  | 100   |
| 40–80   | 60  | 20 | 1200  |
| 80–120  | 100 | 40 | 4000  |
| 120–160 | 140 | 45 | 6300  |
| 160–200 | 180 | 10 | 1800  |
| 200–240 | 220 | 5  | 1100  |
| Total   |     | 125 | 14 500 |

(b)  Mean 116 seconds

## E Averages can mislead

**E1** This question will require a good deal of discussion.

**E2** (a) No, there are two distinct groups – adults and children.
(b) 8·95 years (to 2 d.p.)

**E3** (a) £330  (b) £462

(c) The median gives a better idea because, apart from five very high earners, the earnings are all in the range £280–£370.
(d) Median  (e) Mean  (f) 5 employees

**E4** (a) 34·5  (b) 28·2 hours
(c) The median gives a better idea because, apart from six batteries, the lifetimes are all in the range 29–42 hours.

# 4 Equations and formulas (1)

This chapter deals with the solution of some types of simple equation, including equations arising from substitution into formulas.

## A Inverse operations and balancing

**A1** (a) 16  (b) 22  (c) 19  (d) 9

**A2** (a) 3·3  (b) 12·1  (c) 3·1  (d) 2·1

**A3** (a) 85  (b) 126  (c) 666  (d) 720

**A4** (a) 5·4  (b) 16·5  (c) 0·63

**A5** (a) 3·4  (b) 104  (c) 79  (d) 99
(e) 1·5  (f) 2·8  (g) 10·5  (h) 8·4
(i) 2·7

## B Equations involving two operations (1)

**B1** (a) 6  (b) 7  (c) 9

**B2** (a) Add 5  (b) 6

**B3** (a) 8  (b) 7  (c) 7  (d) 7  (e) 6  (f) 9

**B4** (a) 12·5  (b) $^-2$  (c) 4·5  (d) 3·5
(e) 0·25  (f) $^-0·4$

## C Equations involving two operations (2)

**C1** (a) 8  (b) 324  (c) 98

**C2** (a) 1334  (b) 56  (c) 24

**C3** (a) 5·2  (b) 224  (c) 1·9 (to 1 d.p.)
(d) 144  (e) 1·5  (f) 10·5  (g) 16·4
(h) 88  (i) 51

## D Equations from formulas

**D1** (a) 100  (b) 11·7

**D2** (a) 18  (b) 7·5

**D3** (a) 73·1  (b) 0·252

**D4** (a) 12  (b) 21

**D5** (a) 14·5 m  (b) 20  (c) 6  (d) 12 m

**D6** (a) 59  (b) 10  (c) 37·8

## E Equations with the unknown on both sides

**E1** 6

**E2** 6

**E3** 3

**E4** 5

**E5** 3

**E6** 8

**E7** 4·5

**E8** $^-2$

**E9** 2·4

**E10** $^-5$

# 5 Angles

After a review of basic angle relationships (angles on a line, angles round a point, angles of a triangle) this chapter goes on to angles made with parallel lines. The terms 'F-angles' and 'Z-angles' are used for corresponding and alternate angles (as in the level 2(e) booklet *Angle relationships*). Also included in the chapter are angles of a quadrilateral, and some work on isosceles triangles, including the explanation for the fact that the angle in a semicircle is a right-angle.

## A  Review of angle relationships

**A1**  $a = 45°$, $b = 80°$, $c = 139°$, $d = 139°$

**A2**  $a = 85°$, $b = 136°$

**A3**  (a)  $a = 130°$, $b = 50°$
(b)  $c = 25°$, $d = 155°$, $e = 155°$
(c)  $f = 105°$, $g = 75°$, $h = 105°$

**A4**  $a = 33°$, $b = 39°$, $c = 109°$,
$d = 26°$

**A5**  (a)  $a = 69°$, $b = 69°$, $c = 62°$
(b)  $d = 61°$, $e = 61°$, $f = 77°$,
$g = 77°$, $h = 28°$

**A6**  (a)  $a = 67°$, $b = 55°$, $c = 58°$
$d = 122°$
(b)  $e = 72°$, $f = 64°$, $g = 116°$

**A7**  (a)

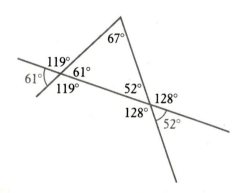

(b)

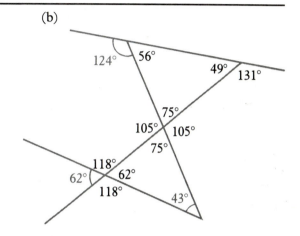

## B  Angles and parallel lines: 'F-angles'

**B1**  (a)  $a = 50°$  (b)  $b = 110°$
(c)  $c = 75°$, $d = 45°$
(d)  $e = 140°$, $f = 115°$

**B2**  (a)  $a = 115°$, $b = 65°$
(b)  $c = 38°$, $d = 142°$, $e = 142°$
(c)  $f = 116°$, $g = 64°$
(d)  $h = 48°$, $i = 48°$, $j = 62°$,
$k = 62°$, $l = 70°$
(d)  $m = 20°$, $n = 35°$, $o = 125°$

## C  Angles and parallel lines: 'Z-angles'

**C1**  (a)  $a = 48°$, $b = 67°$, $c = 65°$
(b)  $d = 100°$, $e = 80°$

## D Calculating angles

**D1** $a = 48°$, $b = 80°$, $c = 48°$

**D2** $a = 72°$, $b = 72°$, $c = 79°$

**D3** $a = 62°$, $b = 50°$, $c = 68°$

**D4** $a = 25°$, $b = 80°$, $c = 114°$

**D5** $a = 145°$, $b = 95°$, $c = 130°$

**D6** (a) $a = 53°$, $b = 127°$, $c = 68°$
  (b) $d = 66°$, $e = 80°$, $f = 34°$
  (c) $g = 39°$, $h = 76°$, $i = 65°$
  (d) $j = 71°$, $k = 71°$, $l = 109°$

## E The angles of a quadrilateral

**E1** (a) $108° + 29° + 43° = 180°$
      $39° + 84° + 57° = 180°$
  (b) $108°$, $113°$, $57°$, $82°$
  (c) The sum of the angles of each triangle is 180°, so the sum of the angles of the quadrilateral is twice 180°, or 360°.

**E2** (a) $a = 65°$, $b = 49°$
  (b) $79° + 99° + 68° + 114° = 360°$

**E3** (a) $a = 140°$
  (b) $b = 126°$, $c = 36°$, $d = 36°$
  (c) $e = 111°$, $f = 69°$, $g = 44°$, $h = 67°$

## F Isosceles triangles; angle in semicircle

**F1** (a) $a = 67°$, $b = 46°$
  (b) $c = d = 11°$
  (c) $e = 38°$, $f = g = 71°$

**F2** (a) $a = 28°$ (b) $b = 37°$

**F3** The angle APB is always about 90°. It is shown on page 33 of the pupil's book that angle APB must always be exactly 90°.

**F4** $a + a+b + b = 180°$
  $2a + 2b = 180°$
  $a + b = 90°$

**F5** (a) $a = 90°$, $b = 33°$
  (b) $c = 90°$, $d = 61°$
  (c) $e = 54°$ (d) $f = 81°$

# 6 Proportionality (1)

This chapter is concerned with the 'multiplier rule': if $Q$ is proportional to $P$, then if $P$ is multiplied by a number, $Q$ is multiplied by the same number. The examples of non-proportionality in section E are not intended as a serious treatment of other kinds of proportionality, merely as a warning that direct proportionality does not always hold.

## A The multiplier rule

**A1** (a) £6 (b) £10 (c) £16 (d) £40

**A2** (a) £8 (b) £16 (c) £40 (d) £80

**A3** (a) 27 tonnes (b) 45 tonnes
  (c) 72 tonnes (d) 90 tonnes
  (e) 900 tonnes

**A4** (a) 28 litres (b) 70 litres
  (c) 700 litres (d) 1400 litres

**A5** (a) (i) 24p (ii) 72p
      (iii) £2·16 (iv) £21·60

  (b) (i) 15cm (ii) 150cm
      (iii) 40cm (iv) 400cm

**A6** (a) £200 (b) £500 (c) £5000
  (d) £25

## B Using a calculator

**B1** (a) 1·9 (b) 285cm

**B2** 200cm

**B3** (a) 0·8 (b) 120cm

**B4** (a) $1 \cdot 32\ldots$  (b) $1138\,$g (to the nearest gram)

**B5** $20 \cdot 6\,$cm (to 1 d.p.)

## C  Scaling up and down

**C1** Sugar $1000\,$g
Milk $2 \cdot 5$ litres

**C2** Flour $5 \cdot 625\,$kg
Eggs 37 or 38

**C3** $11 \cdot 7\,$kg (to 1 d.p.)

**C4** The answer is the same.

## D  Non-proportionality

**D1** $\dfrac{25}{16} = 1 \cdot 5625$  $\dfrac{64 \cdot 9}{17 \cdot 0} = 3 \cdot 8176$ (both to 4 d.p.)

**D2** (a) The pupil's own calculation should indicate that the depth multiplier is not the same as the volume multiplier.
(b) No. See page 40.

**D3** (a)

| Length in cm | 1 | 2 | 3 | 4 | 5 | 6 |
|---|---|---|---|---|---|---|
| Area in cm² | 1 | 4 | 9 | 16 | 25 | 36 |

(b) No  (c) No

**D4**

| Length in cm | 1 | 2 | 3 | 4 | 5 | 6 |
|---|---|---|---|---|---|---|
| Perimeter in cm | 4 | 8 | 12 | 16 | 20 | 24 |

The perimeter is proportional to the length of the side. If, for instance, you double the length of the side, the perimeter is doubled also.

**D5**

| Length in cm | 1 | 2 | 3 | 4 | 5 | 6 |
|---|---|---|---|---|---|---|
| Volume in cm³ | 1 | 8 | 27 | 64 | 125 | 216 |

No, volume is not proportional to the length of edge. If, for instance, you double the length of each edge, you do not double the volume.

**D6** No, the length is not proportional to the weight. For instance, 40 to 60 clearly does not have the same multiplier as $3 \cdot 5$ to $8 \cdot 5$.

---

# 7  Equations and formulas (2)

This chapter is about re-arranging formulas, thought of in a similar way to solving equations.

## A  Equations from formulas

**A1** (a) $85 = 34b$
(b) $\dfrac{85}{34} = \dfrac{34b}{34}$  so  $b = 2 \cdot 5$
(c) $28 = 35a$  (d) $a = 0 \cdot 8$

**A2** (a) $23 = 4q + 11$
(b) $23 - 11 = 4q + 11 - 11$
$12 = 4q$
so  $q = 3$
(c) $17 = 2p + 10$  (d) $p = 3 \cdot 5$

## B  Re-arranging a formula

**B1** (a) $d = st$
$\dfrac{d}{t} = \dfrac{st}{t}$
so $s = \dfrac{d}{t}$
(b) $s = 0 \cdot 35$

**B2** (a) $w = \dfrac{f}{n}$  (b) $n = \dfrac{f}{w}$

**B3** $p = \dfrac{q}{5}$

**B4**    $m = \dfrac{c}{n}$

**B5**    $b = \dfrac{c}{3a}$

**B6**    $x = y - c$

**B7**    $r = s + b$

**B8**    $v = w - u$

**B9**    $x = y - 7$

**B10**    (a) $V = IR$    (b) $V = 3\cdot6$

**B11**    (a) $x = y - a$    (b) $x = yb$

      (c) $x = y + c$    (d) $x = \dfrac{y}{d}$

      (e) $x = y - e$

## C   Further re-arrangements

**C1**    $x = \dfrac{y - b}{a}$

**C2**    $r = \dfrac{s + d}{c}$

**C3**    (a) $p = \dfrac{q - a}{4}$    (b) $p = \dfrac{q - a}{k}$

      (c) $k = \dfrac{q - a}{p}$    (d) $p = \dfrac{q - k}{a}$

(e) $f = \dfrac{m + t}{a}$    (f) $v = \dfrac{w - u}{k}$

(g) $u = \dfrac{w + v}{k}$    (h) $k = \dfrac{w - u}{v}$

(i) $m = \dfrac{t + n}{p}$

**C4**    $s = p(k + a)$

**C5**    $c = n(d - a)$

**C6**    (a) $x = p(q + r)$    (b) $x = p(r - q)$

      (c) $x = r(p - q)$

## D   Mixed examples

**D1**    $v = mu$

**D2**    (a) $w = \dfrac{l - b}{a}$    (b) $a = \dfrac{l - b}{w}$

**D3**    (a) $x = \dfrac{w + d}{c}$    (b) $c = \dfrac{w + d}{x}$

**D4**    $t = 3(s - f)$

**D5**    $x = 4(y + a)$

**D6**    $x = 3u - w$

**D7**    $x = t(q + s)$

# 8   Gradient

The gradient of a hill or slope is introduced, first as a percentage, then as a decimal. (The form '1 in $n$' is not used.)

## A   Steepness

**A1**    (a) 20m    (b) 60m    (c) 8m
      (d) 12m    (e) 18m

**A2**    (a) 12m    (b) 36m    (c) 4·8m
      (d) 7·2m    (e) 10·8m
      (f) No, it is less steep.

**A3**    (a) 0·15    (b) 0·17    (c) 0·07    (d) 0·3

**A4**    (a) 28m    (b) 38·4m    (c) 80m

**A5**    (a) 168m    (b) 277·2m    (c) 195·2m

**A6**    (a) 30·9m    (b) 86·9m

**A7**    210m

**A8**    7·2m

**A9**    (a) 3·7m    (b) 45°

## B Calculating gradients

**B1** 0·15

**B2** (a) Gradient A, 0·18; gradient B, 0·16
(b) Hill A is steeper.

**B3** 3·5

**B4** (a) $\dfrac{27}{75} = 0·36$

(b) $\dfrac{34}{95} = 0·36$ (to 2 d.p.)

(c) $\dfrac{16}{44} = 0·36$ (to 2 d.p.)

**B5** 0·63 (to 2 d.p.)

**B6** (a) 0·11, rack and pinion (train)
(b) 0·43, rack and pinion (single car)
(c) 0·75, funicular
(d) 0·07, ordinary

---

# Review 1

---

## 1 Using a calculator

**1.1** (a) 73·08 (b) 0·44 (c) 5·62

**1.2** No, the result is 23·81 (to 2 d.p.).

**1.3** 2·0038

## 3 Averages

**3.1** (a) 52·1 kg (b) 51·3 kg
(c) The netball team is heavier, on average.

**3.2**

| Number of peas in pod | Frequency | Number of peas in group |
|---|---|---|
| 4 | 8 | 32 |
| 5 | 11 | 55 |
| 6 | 16 | 96 |
| 7 | 10 | 70 |
| Total | 45 | 253 |

Mean number of peas in pod = 5·6

**3.3** (a) 0·5 kg

(b)

| Weight in kg | Mid-interval value | Frequency | Weight of group, in kg |
|---|---|---|---|
| 0–1 | 0·5 | 1 | 0·5 |
| 1–2 | 1·5 | 6 | 9·0 |
| 2–3 | 2·5 | 10 | 25·0 |
| 3–4 | 3·5 | 13 | 45·5 |
| 4–5 | 4·5 | 7 | 31·5 |
| Total | | 37 | 111·5 |

Mean weight 3·0 kg (approx.)

## 4 Equations and formulas (1)

**4.1** (a) 8 (b) 17 (c) 325

**4.2** (a) ⁻58·7 (b) 1·31 (to 2 d.p.)

**4.3** (a) 3 (b) 3 (c) 8 (d) 1·304
(e) 0·36

## 5 Angles

**5.1** (a) $a = 40°$
(b) $b = 62°$, $c = 74°$, $d = 106°$
(c) $e = 39°$, $f = 39°$, $g = 141°$
(d) $h = 44°$

**5.2** (a) $a = 125°$ (b) $b = 74°$
(c) $c = 90°$, $d = 36°$

## 6 Proportionality (1)

**6.1** (a) £37·50 (b) £60 (c) £600
(d) £750 (e) £7500

**6.2** 2·24 ohms

**6.3** 128 kg

**6.4** 16·7 cm

## 7 Equations and formulas (2)

**7.1** $V = RT$

**7.2** (a) $r = p - 2q$ (b) $q = \dfrac{p - r}{2}$

**7.3** (a) $q = p + s$ (b) $q = \dfrac{p + s}{a}$
(c) $a = \dfrac{p + s}{q}$ (d) $x = \dfrac{y - b}{a}$
(e) $a = \dfrac{y - b}{x}$ (f) $b = y - ax$
(g) $l = zd$ (h) $a = f(m - b)$
(i) $x = k(y + a)$

## 8 Gradient

**8.1** (a) 90 m (b) 27 m (c) 24·75 m (d) 81 m

**8.2** (a) 0·46 (b) 0·36

**8.3** 0·43

**8.4** 8·05 m

## M Miscellaneous

**M1** (a) Pupil's estimate
(b) Coloured rectangle 18 cm$^2$
Rectangle ABCD 28 cm$^2$
(c) 64% (to the nearest %)

# 9 In your head (2)

This chapter consists of questions on multiplication and division, to be done mentally.

## Multiplication and division

**1** (a) 12 (b) 20 (c) 18 (d) 27
(e) 40 (f) 49 (g) 32 (h) 36
(i) 35 (j) 36 (k) 25 (l) 28

**2** (a) 24 (b) 30 (c) 14 (d) 64
(e) 21 (f) 18 (g) 16 (h) 45
(i) 24 (j) 15 (k) 42 (l) 72

**3** (a) 10 (b) 8 (c) 2 (d) 6
(e) 6 (f) 6

**4** (a) 8 (b) 3 (c) 5 (d) 9
(e) 4 (f) 10 (g) 7 (h) 8
(i) 4 (j) 5 (k) 6 (l) 4
(m) 2 (n) 8

**5** (a) 120 (b) 80 (c) 150 (d) 240
(e) 210 (f) 320 (g) 180 (h) 180
(i) 200 (j) 300 (k) 240 (l) 280

**6** (a) 65 (b) 72 (c) 84 (d) 98
(e) 90 (f) 140 (g) 84 (h) 51
(i) 96 (j) 96 (k) 98 (l) 64

# 10   Equations and formulas (3)

Formulas of the types $A = BC$ and $A = \dfrac{B}{C}$ arise often in science. This chapter deals with the different kinds of calculation and re-arrangement they can give rise to, including the 'difficult case' of using $A = \dfrac{B}{C}$ to find $C$ given $A$ and $B$, or to express $C$ in terms of $A$ and $B$.

## A   The density formula

**A1**   (a) $12\,\text{cm}^3$   (b) $8\cdot9\,\text{g}$
          (c) $8\cdot9\,\text{g per cm}^3$

**A2**   $7\cdot9\,\text{g per cm}^3$

**A3**   (a) $7\cdot9\,\text{g per cm}^3$   (b) $11\cdot3\,\text{g per cm}^3$
          (c) $7\cdot1\,\text{g per cm}^3$

## B   Using $D = \dfrac{M}{V}$ to calculate $M$ or $V$

**B1**   28

**B2**   119

**B3**   $1\cdot5$. Working should be shown as on page 57 of the pupil's book. Also a check should be shown.

**B4**   15

**B5**   (a) 12   (b) $1\cdot7$   (c) 7

**B6**   $7\cdot5$

**B7**   12

**B8**   $0\cdot026$

**B9**   $0\cdot625$

## C   Miscellaneous calculations from formulas

**C1**   (a) $1\cdot6$   (b) $5\cdot8$

**C2**   (a) 32   (b) $5\cdot7$

**C3**   (a) 53   (b) 5

**C4**   (a) $4\cdot8$   (b) 4100   (c) 5700

## D   Re-arranging formulas

**D1**   $V = IR$

**D2**   $R = \dfrac{V}{I}$

**D3**   (a) $m = lnz$   (b) $z = \dfrac{m}{ln}$

   (c) $e = \dfrac{acx}{b}$   (d) $x = \dfrac{be}{ac}$

   (e) $R = \dfrac{PT}{F}$   (f) $n = \dfrac{A}{5f}$

   (g) $F = \dfrac{YAe}{l}$   (h) $A = \dfrac{Fl}{Ye}$

   (i) $a = \dfrac{vsx}{2t}$

# 11 Area

This chapter covers the area of the parallelogram, triangle and trapezium. The more usual explanation of the rule for the area of a parallelogram, shown in the sequence of diagrams below, breaks down when the 'top' of the parallelogram completely overhangs the base.

  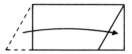

## A  The area of a parallelogram

The answers to questions in this section are dependent on measuring.

**A1**  (a)  Base (AB) 4·7 cm
Height    2·8 cm
Area    13 cm² (to nearest cm²)
(b)  Base (BC) 3·4 cm
Height    3·9 cm
Area    13 cm² (to nearest cm²)

**A2**  (a)  12 cm²  (b)  22 cm²  (c)  37 cm²
(all to nearest cm²)

**A3**  (a)  21 square units
(b)  14 square units
(c)  30 square units
Some pupils will need to be reminded of the need to draw diagrams for parts (b) and (c).

**A4**  Answers in the range 13·3 cm² – 14·0 cm², dependent on measuring

## B  The area of a triangle

**B1**  (a)  Base (AB) 4·1 cm
Height    5·3 cm
Area    11 cm² (to nearest cm²)
(b)  Base (BC) 5·7 cm
Height    3·8 cm
Area    11 cm² (to nearest cm²)
(c)  Base (AC) 8·2 cm
Height    2·6 cm
Area    11 cm² (to nearest cm²)

**B2**  (a)  20 cm²  (b)  28 cm²
(both to nearest cm²)

**B3**  (a)  12·5 square units
(b)  7 square units
(c)  10·5 square units
Some pupils will need to be reminded of the need to draw diagrams for parts (b) and (c).

**B4**  (a)  14 cm  (b)  140 m  (c)  34 m
(d)  2380 m²  (e)  2240 m²  (f)  4620 m²

**B5**  Field A    6200 m²
Field B    9000 m²
Field C  13 300 m²
(all to nearest 100 m²)

## C  Drawing a triangle given the lengths of its sides

The following answers have been calculated to 3 s.f.

**C1**  (a), (b)  Pupil's scale drawing
(c)  1770 cm²

**C2**  (a)  15·0 cm²  (b)  13·4 cm²

**C3**  (a)  Pupil's scale drawing
(b)  There are several ways the shed will fit. Check by measuring.
(c)  1740 m²

## D   The area of a trapezium

**D1**   B, D and E are trapeziums.

**D2**   (a) 306 cm²   (b) 12·8 cm² (to 1 d.p.)

**D3**   22·6 m²

**D4**   (a) A, 76·1 m²; B, 30 m²;
            C, 77·9 m²; D, 21·6 m²
            (b) 206 m²   (c) £1340
            (all to 3 s.f.)

**D5**   218·2 m²

**D6**   744 m² (to nearest m²)

---

# 12   Proportionality (2)

This chapter deals with three further aspects of proportionality: if $Q$ is proportional to $P$ then (1) the graph of $(P, Q)$ is a straight line through $(0, 0)$; (2) the ratio $\dfrac{Q}{P}$ is constant; (3) this ratio is equal to the gradient of the graph. Section D is concerned with 'approximate proportionality', important in interpreting experimental data.

---

## A   Proportionality and graphs

**A1**   (a)

| Length in cm | 0 | 5 | 10 | 15 | 20 | 25 |
|---|---|---|---|---|---|---|
| Cost in pence | 0 | 8 | 16 | 24 | 32 | 40 |

(b)  See the graph on page 70.

**A2**   (a)

| Area in m² | 0 | 4 | 8 | 12 | 16 | 20 | 24 | 28 |
|---|---|---|---|---|---|---|---|---|
| Cost in £ | 0 | 3 | 6 | 9 | 12 | 15 | 18 | 21 |

(b)

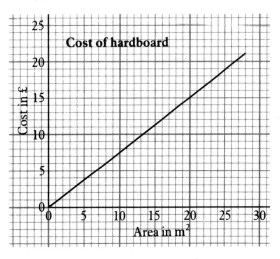

(c)  £18·75 (calculated)

**A3** (a)

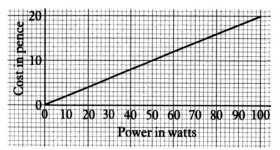

(b) (i) 5p (ii) 8p (iii) 12p
(c) 30p

**A4** (a)

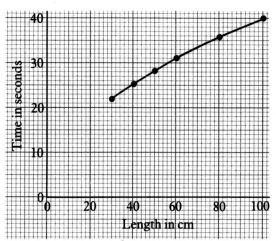

(b) No, the time for 20 swings is not proportional to the length.

# B The constant ratio rule

**B1** (a)

| Width in mm | 20 | 25 | 30 | 40 | 50 |
|---|---|---|---|---|---|
| Height in mm | 28 | 35 | 42 | 56 | 70 |

(The second width may be measured as 24 mm.)
(b) All the ratios are equal to 1·4.

**B2** (a)

| Height in m | 5 | 10 | 15 | 20 | 25 |
|---|---|---|---|---|---|
| Shadow length in m | 8 | 16 | 24 | 32 | 40 |

(b) All the ratios are equal to 1·6.
(c) 20·8 m

**B3** (a) The current is proportional to the voltage. The constant ratio is 2·4.
(b)

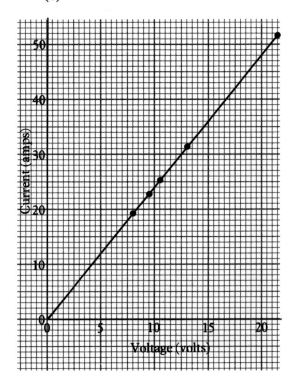

**B4** (a) Weight is not proportional to the diameter. The ratios are not constant.

(b) The graph is not a straight line through (0,0).

*(b)*

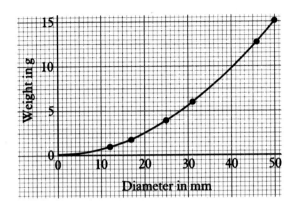

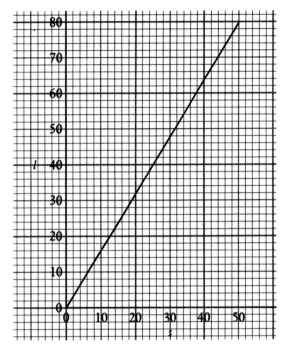

## C  Gradient

**C1** (a)
| $h$ | 5 | 10 | 15 | 20 | 25 |
|---|---|---|---|---|---|
| $s$ | 15 | 30 | 45 | 60 | 75 |

(b) $\dfrac{s}{h} = 3$ for each pair in the table

(c) Yes  (d) 1·6  (e) $l = 1\cdot6s$

**C2** (a) 2·5  (b) $E = 2\cdot5m$  (c) 0·8
(d) $E = 0\cdot8m$
(e) (i) 625 calories  (ii) 200 calories

**C3** (a)
| $s$ | 20 | 25 | 35 | 45 |
|---|---|---|---|---|
| $l$ | 32 | 40 | 56 | 72 |

**C4** (a)
| Rectangle | A | B | C | D |
|---|---|---|---|---|
| $s$ | 30 | 42 | 50 | 70 |
| $l$ | 36 | 54 | 60 | 84 |

(b)

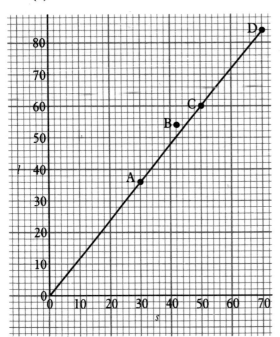

Rectangle B is the odd one out.
(c) $l = 1 \cdot 2s$
(d) $1 \cdot 29$ (to 3 s.f.)

**C5** (a)

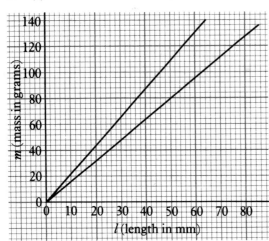

(b) $m = 1 \cdot 6l$ and $m = 2 \cdot 2l$. The second represents the thicker wire.

**D  Approximate proportionality**

**D1** (a) $1 \cdot 6$, $1 \cdot 8$, $1 \cdot 67$, $1 \cdot 75$, $1 \cdot 74$, $1 \cdot 67$
   (b) Three are greater than $1 \cdot 7$, and three are less than $1 \cdot 7$. Pupils should be asked how this answer relates to the graph on page 77 of the pupil's book.

**D2** (a) and (b)

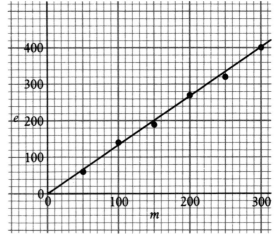

(c) Gradient $1 \cdot 3$ (to 2 s.f.), $e = 1 \cdot 3m$

**D3** (a)

| $m$ | 10 | 20 | 30 | 40 | 50 |
|---|---|---|---|---|---|
| $e$ | 14 | 25 | 42 | 52 | 63 |

   (b)

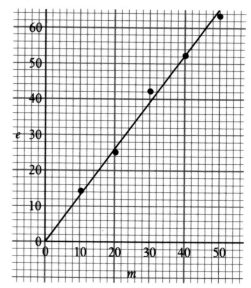

(c) Gradient $1 \cdot 3$ (to 2 s.f.), $e = 1 \cdot 3m$

20

**D4** (a)

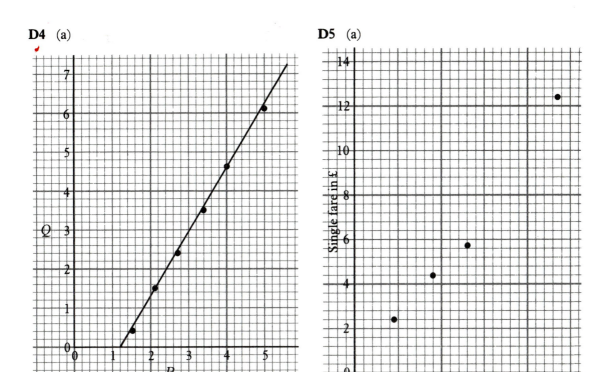

(b) $Q$ is not proportional to $P$.

**D5** (a)

(b) No  (c) Newbury  (d) Westbury

# 13  On paper (1)

The skills of pencil-and-paper arithmetic required for the work in this short chapter and in chapter 22 extend to addition, subtraction, multiplication by 2, 3, 4, ..., up to 9, and division by 2, 3, 4, ..., up to 9, applied to whole numbers and money.

1  (a) 806  (b) 923  (c) 3192  (d) £8·91
(e) £20·29  (f) £84·75

2  (a) 226  (b) 241  (c) 609  (d) 1017
(e) 406  (f) 628

3  (a) 3805  (b) 1692  (c) 2046  (d) 5448
(e) 5370  (f) 1638

4  (a) 91  (b) 236  (c) 74  (d) 173
(e) 804  (f) 708

5  £14·40

6  £2·67

7  £14·55

8  £1·45

9  £20·33

10  66 eggs each, 6 eggs left over

# 14 Plans and elevations

Different methods of representing three-dimensional objects have different uses. Plans and elevations allow measurements to be taken from drawings and are used by architects, engineers, craft-workers and others. (A full treatment of the topic would be inappropriate in this context; there is for example no mention of the correct positioning and alignment of views.)

## A Getting measurements from drawings

**A1** (a) A, B or C, 1·7 cm
(b) A or C, 2·1 cm
(c) A, B or C, 1·2 cm
(d) A or C, 8·1 cm

**A2**

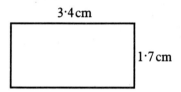

3·4 cm

1·7 cm

**A3** A, H, F; D, K, L; G, B, E; J, C, I

**A4** A, J, P; B, I, T; D, E, K; F, H, O; G, M, Q; L, C, S; U, N, R

## B Buildings

**B1** (a) Plan view (b) 6·5 m (c) 3·1 m
(d) 5·5 m (e)

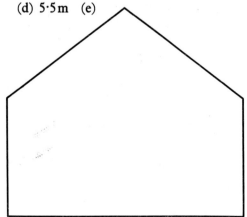

(f) 4·0 m (g) 86 m² (to 2 s.f.)

**B2** (a) 15·5 m² (b) 16·5 m² (c) 9·6 m²

**B3** (a) Elevation C (b) Elevation A
(c)

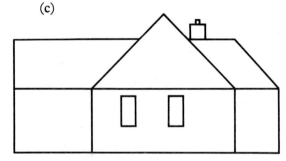

(d) Two (e) (i) Back bedroom
(ii) Dining room (iii) Kitchen
(iv) Lounge

# 15 Rates

Starting with constant rates, this chapter moves on to average rates and to values of average rates calculated from graphs.

## A  Constant rates

**A1**  (a) 10 litre/min  (b) 67 litre/min
    (c) 12 litre/min  (d) 7 litre/min

**A2**  52 500 litres

**A3**  0·33 litre/min

**A4**  (a)

| Time in minutes | 0 | 0·5 | 1 | 1·5 | 2 | 3 | 4 | 5 |
|---|---|---|---|---|---|---|---|---|
| Amount in litres | 0 | 7 | 14 | 21 | 28 | 42 | 56 | 70 |

(b)

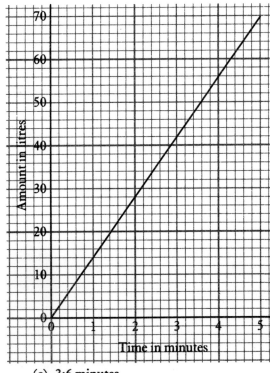

(c) 3·6 minutes

**A5**  62·5 litre/min

**A6**  (a) 15 litre/min  (b) 0·3125 litre/min
    (c) 7·5 litre/min  (d) 0·05 litre/min

**A7**  217 m/s

**A8**  6·5 m/s

**A9**  (a) 1·27 dollars per pound
    (b) 0·79 pounds per dollar

**A10**  £2·75 per hour

**A11**  63 pence per hour

**A12**  (a) 8 grams per $cm^3$   (b) Density

**A13**  Each square metre weighs 50 grams.

## B  Average rates

**B1**  56·1 miles per hour

**B2**  47·7 miles per hour

**B3**  (a) 0·78 hour  (b) 6·47 hours
    (c) 2·12 hours

**B4**  73·5 miles per hour

**B5**  11·41 litre/100 km

**B6**  19·22 litre/100 km

**B7**  (a) 0·86 hundred km
    (b) 11·63 litre/100 km
    (c) 9·14 litre/100 km

## C  Changes in rates

**C1**  (a) 20 litre/min  (b) 4 litre/min
    (c) 10 litre/min

**C2**  (a) 1·6 km/min  (b) 4 km/min
    (c) 1 km/min

**C3**  (a) 250 km/h  (b) 550 km/h
    (c) 200 km/h

**C4**  1·9 km/min

**C5**  (a) 180 km  (b) 7 hours  (c) 25·7 km/h

**C6** (a) 63·6km/h  (b) 47·4km/h  
(c) 44·5km/h  (d) 50·4km/h

**C7** (a) 3 degrees/min  (b) 2 degrees/min  
(c) 1·5 degrees/min  (d) 1 degree/min  
(e) 0·5 degree/min

**C8** (a) 120m  (b) 12m/s  
(c) (i) 23m/s  (ii) 20m/s  (iii) 3·33m/s  
(d) 12·5m/s

**C9** (a) (i) 26·67 degrees/min  
(ii) 22 degrees/min  
(iii) 9·5 degrees/min  
(b) (i) 24 degrees/min  
(ii) 16 degrees/min  
(iii) 10·67 degrees/min

**D  Calculations with rates**

**D1** (a) 9 min  (b) 27 litres

**D2** 6·5 hours

**D3** 4 hours

**D4** (a) 58g  (b) 0·22 litre

**D5** 140 metres

**D6** (a) 600 cubic metres  
(b) In about 23 days

**D7** $2 \times 10^9$

**D8** 133·2g of glucose per litre

**D9** 4·8 litres per hour

**D10** 1·36 minutes

# Review 2

## 10  Equations and formulas (3)

**10.1** (a) 160  (b) 7·3

**10.2** (a) 0·37  (b) 8·8

**10.3** (a) $a = \dfrac{cd}{b}$  (b) $c = \dfrac{ab}{d}$

## 11  Area

**11.1** (a) 26·52cm$^2$  (b) 9·9cm$^2$  
(c) 50·88cm$^2$  (d) 36·54cm$^2$

**11.2** 40·5m$^2$

## 12  Proportionality (2)

**12.1** (a) 76·9 litres  (b) 292·5m$^2$

**12.2** (a) 0·6  (b) $Q = 0·6P$

**12.3** (a), (b), (c)

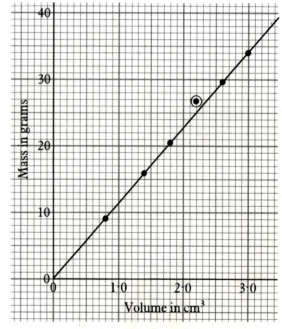

(d) About 11·3  
(e) The density of lead is 11·3 grams per cm$^3$.

## 14 Plans and elevations

**14.1** A, G, R; F, N, Q; K, E, I;
L, B, H; O, C, J; P, D, M

**14.2** 4500 cm² or 4600 cm² (to 2 s.f.)

**14.3**

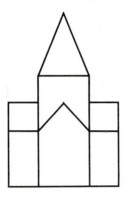

## 15 Rates

**15.1** (a) 1·2 litres per second
(b) 72 litres per minute

**15.2** Standard 3·62 hours per penny
Super    4·48 hours per penny
**or**
Standard 0·276p per hour
Super    0·223p per hour
So the Super is better value.

**15.3** (a) 5·2 grams   (b) 3·2 hours

**15.4** (a) 254 yen per dollar
(b) 0·003 94 dollars per yen
(both to 3 s.f.)

**15.5** (a) 10 deg/min   (b) About 1·6 deg/min

## M Miscellaneous

**M1** (a) 5·4 cm   (b) 4·4 cm   (c) 2·8 cm
(all to 1 d.p.)

**M2** 6%

---

# 16  Simplifying expressions

Sections A, B and C deal with simple cases of 'collecting terms' (e.g. simplifying $2a + 3 + 5a - 7$).  Section D deals with simplifying expressions involving mutiplication, such as $2ab \times 3a$.

---

## A  Order of adding and subtracting

**A1** (a) Yes, 88   (b) Pupil's own choice
(c) Yes  (d) Yes

**A2** (b) and (d) are equivalent.

**A3** There are five other expressions, including the two already found in A2.
$w - x + z - y$
$w - y - x + z$
$w - y + z - x$
$w + z - x - y$
$w + z - y - x$

## B  Simplifying expressions (1)

**B1** (a) $(3 \times 5) - 2 + (4 \times 5) + 7 = 40$
$(7 \times 5) + 5 = 40$ ✔
(b) $(3 \times 9) - 2 + (4 \times 9) + 7 = 68$
$(7 \times 9) + 5 = 68$ ✔

**B2**     $6n + 3 - 2n + 4$
$= 6n - 2n + 3 + 4$
$= \quad 4n \quad + \quad 7$

**B3** (a) $6n - 7$
(b) $(4 \times 10) - 2 - 5 + (2 \times 10) = 53$
$(6 \times 10) - 7 = 53$ ✔

**B4** (a) $3n + 5$   (b) $8n + 5$   (c) $12n - 10$
(d) $7n + 2$   (e) $8n - 6$   (f) $8n + 5$

**B5** (a) $7 + 9n$   (b) $3 + 2n$   (c) $10 + 2n$
(d) $14 - 5n$   (e) $2 + 4n$   (f) $4 + n$

**B6** (a) $5n - 7$   (b) $11 + 2n$   (c) $2n + 2$
(d) $1 - 4n$   (e) $5 - 2n$   (f) $3n + 5$

25

**B7**  $^-2 + 6n$

**B8**  (a) $^-4 + 2n$  (b) $^-2n + 5$  (c) $2p - 4$
(d) $^-2x + 1$  (e) $^-1 + 4y$  (f) $^-4z - 8$

## C  Equations

**C1**  (a) 4
(b) $(5 \times 4) - 6 - (2 \times 4) + 4 = 10$ ✔

**C2**  (a) 2  (b) 3  (c) 3  (d) 3  (e) 2  (f) 4

**C3**  (a) 2  (b) 1  (c) 4  (d) 4

**C4**  (a) 4  (b) 4

**C5**  B has $2x + 5\frac{1}{2}$,
C has $6x + 20$,
D has $24x + 84\frac{1}{2}$.
$x + 1\frac{1}{2} + 2x + 5\frac{1}{2} + 6x + 20 + 24x + 84\frac{1}{2} = 144\frac{1}{2}$
$x = 1$
So A has $2\frac{1}{2}$, B $7\frac{1}{2}$, C 26 and D $108\frac{1}{2}$.

## D  Simplifying expressions (2)

**D1**  (a) $8xy$  (b) $10pq$  (c) $12ab$
(d) $12abc$  (e) $6xyz$  (f) $12pqr$
(g) $6abc$  (h) $15xyz$  (i) $8abc$

**D2**  (a) $6x^2$  (b) $8xy^2$  (c) $3a^2b$
(d) $20ab^2$  (e) $3p^2q$  (f) $20b^2c$
(g) $21ab^2$  (h) $20x^2$  (i) $6pq^2$

**★D3**  (a) $a^7$  (b) $a^8$  (c) $a^{10}$
Add the indices.
$a^{19} \times a^{27} = a^{46}$

# 17  In your head (3)

## Decimals, percentages and fractions

1  (a) 4·8  (b) 5·1  (c) 7·3  (d) 10·2

2  (a) 5·2  (b) 2·8  (c) 3·8  (d) 0·4

3  (a) 6·5  (b) 60·5  (c) 31·85  (d) 0·55
(e) 32·95  (f) 21·925  (g) 51·05  (h) 0·05

4  (a) 7·02  (b) 24·51  (c) 0·06  (d) 124·76

5  (a) £6  (b) £6·40  (c) 64p
(d) 83p  (e) £11·27

6  40%

7  63%

8  27%

9  (a) 9  (b) 27  (c) 46  (d) 16
(e) 36  (f) 45  (g) 120  (h) 15

10  (a) (i) 0·5  (ii) 50%
(b) (i) 0·25  (ii) 25%
(c) (i) 0·75  (ii) 75%
(d) (i) 0·2  (ii) 20%
(e) (i) 0·6  (ii) 60%
(f) (i) 0·7  (ii) 70%
(g) (i) 0·09  (ii) 9%

11  0·035, 0·08, 0·308, 0·37, 0·41, 0·57, 1·06

# 18 Contours

After explaining what contour lines are, this chapter gives some questions involving the interpretation of contour maps.

## A Heights above sea-level

**A1** The contours are more spaced out on the left-hand part, so the land must rise less quickly.

**A2** (a) Path from A  (b) Path from C

**A3** (a) 200m  (b) Downhill  (c) Uphill
(d) From left to right

**A4** (a) 300m, 250m, 250m, 300m
(b) Go downhill first, then uphill

**A5** (a) Go downhill first, then uphill
(b) Go downhill all the way
(c) Go uphill all the way

(d) Go downhill first, then uphill
(e) Go downhill all the way

## B Contours on OS maps

**B1** 90m

**B2** Uphill

**B3** Driving from 510430, you go downhill for about 2km, then rise slightly as you pass the second milestone, then downhill again.

**B4** About 85 m above sea-level

**B5** 490408; about 70m above sea-level

# 19 Brackets

This chapter is concerned with multiplying out brackets in expressions such as $3(a + b)$ and the reverse process of factorisation.

## A Multiplying out brackets (1)

**A1** (a) $c + d + c + d + c + d$
(b) $3c + 3d$  (c) $3(c + d)$

**A2** (a) $7r + 7s$  (b) $6a + 6b$
(c) $10e + 10f$  (d) $8l + 8m + 8n$

**A3** $3(50 + 7) = 150 + 21 = 171$

**A4** (a) 215  (b) 192  (c) 192  (d) 344

**A5** (a) $5s + 5t$  (b) $2u + 2v + 2w$
(c) $9f + 9g + 9h + 9i$

**A6** (a) $6a + 2b$  (b) $5p + 15q$
(c) $6p + 6q$  (d) $8a + 12b$
(e) $18a + 24b$  (f) $40r + 20s$
(g) $3a + 6b + 9c$  (h) $8p + 4q + 12r$
(i) $30a + 18b + 6c$
(j) $16a + 8b + 24c + 32d$

**A7** (a) $12x + 6$  (b) $24 + 12p$
(c) $20r + 15$  (d) $14 + 6y$
(e) $8a + 40$  (f) $18a + 6$
(g) $30a + 80$  (h) $35 + 14c$

## B Multiplying out brackets (2)

**B1** (a) $3s - 3t$  (b) $5a - 5b$  (c) $4p - 4q$
(d) $6a - 4$  (e) $15 - 12r$  (f) $16p - 24q$
(g) $6a + 6b - 6c$  (h) $5a - 10b + 15c$
(i) $8a - 12b - 8$  (j) $30a + 10b - 50$

## C Equations with brackets

**C1** 9

**C2** 8

**C3** 12

**C4** 6

**C5** (a) 2   (b) 10

**C6** 14

**C7** 5

**C8** 7

**\*C9** (a) 13
(b) Sarah will be 26, and her mother 52.

**\*C10** (a) $8 + y$   (b) $32 + y$
(c) $3(8 + y) = 32 + y$
(d) $y = 4$, so Olav will be 12 and his
   father 36.
(e) It checks.

**\*C11** (a) (i) $40 + x$ litres   (ii) $15 + x$ litres
(b) $40 + x = 2(15 + x)$
(c) $x = 10$
   So vat A contains 50 litres, vat B 25 litres.
(d) It checks.

**\*C12** $x = 20$, so vat A contains 70 litres,
vat B 35 litres.

## D  Multiplying out brackets (3)

**D1** (a) $xy + xz$   (b) $fg - fh$   (c) $3s + st$
(d) $ap + aq - ar$

**D2** (a) $a^2 + 4a$   (b) $3x + xy$   (c) $uv - uw$
(d) $ab - a^2$   (e) $p^2 + 3pq$   (f) $2r^2 - rs$
(g) $2a + a^2$   (h) $5x - 2x^2$   (i) $2m^2 + mn$
(j) $3x^2 + x$   (k) $2a^2 + 6ab$   (l) $12x - 9x^2$

**D3** (a) $a + 2b$   (b) $2a(a + 2b)$   (c) $2a^2 + 4ab$
(d) The $2a^2$ represents the two top panels; the
   $4ab$ represents the four bottom panels.

## E  Factorising

**E1** (b) $2(a + b)$   (c) $7(x + y)$
(d) $9(a - b)$   (e) $4(m - n)$
(f) $3(p + q - r)$

**E2** (a) $5(x + 2)$   (b) $3(3x - 5)$
(c) $2(3a - 4b)$   (d) $6(5 + 2q)$

**E3** (a) $2(3x + 5)$   (b) $3(3y + 4)$
(c) $3(p - 10)$   (d) $7(2a - 3b)$
(e) $2(4s - 5t)$   (f) $3(2f + 3g)$
(g) $2(9 - 2q)$   (h) $5(5x + 8y)$
(i) $2(7 + 8p)$   (j) $5(4 - q)$
(k) $5(4x + 3)$   (l) $5(6a - 5b)$

**E4** (a) $4(a + 3b)$   (b) $4(5x - 3y)$
(c) $6(x + 3y)$   (d) $4(3a + 4b)$
(e) $4(6 + 5p)$   (f) $10(3a - 4)$
(g) $8(x - 3y)$   (h) $4(7x - 9y)$

**E5** (a) $r(2 + s)$   (b) $a(3 + b)$
(c) $x(y + 5)$   (d) $2a(1 + 2b)$
(e) $3x(2 + 3y)$   (f) $a(x + y)$
(g) $5(px + qy)$   (h) $2a(2x + 3y)$

**E6** (a) There are two walls each of area
   $lh$ and two of area $bh$. So the
   total area to be painted is $2lh + 2bh$.
(b) $2h(l + b)$

# 20  Probability

Probability was first introduced in *Book B2*, through the idea of relative
frequency. (See the note on chapter 14 of *Book B2*.) This chapter
introduces the idea of equally likely outcomes.

## A  Random selection

**A1** $\frac{3}{50}$ or $0.06$

**A2** (a) $\frac{1}{40}$,  $0.025$   (b) $\frac{7}{40}$,  $0.175$
(c) $\frac{7}{400}$, $0.0175$   (d) $\frac{3}{1000}$, $0.003$
(e) $\frac{1}{65}$, $0.0154$ (to 3 s.f.)
(f) $\frac{9}{65}$, $0.138$ (to 3 s.f.)
(g) $\frac{1}{100}$, $0.01$   (h) $\frac{1}{100}$, $0.01$

**A3** (a) $\frac{1}{20}$, $0.05$   (b) $\frac{19}{20}$, $0.95$

**A4** (a) $\frac{1}{6}$   (b) $\frac{2}{3}$   (c) $\frac{1}{3}$

**A5** (a) $\frac{1}{8}$   (b) $\frac{3}{8}$   (c) $\frac{1}{2}$   (d) $\frac{1}{8}$

**A6** $\frac{15}{80} = \frac{3}{16}$

## B  Probability

**B1**  $\frac{3}{4}$

**B2**  $\frac{3}{8}$

**B3**  (a) $\frac{1}{4}$  (b) $\frac{3}{8}$  (c) $\frac{1}{2}$

**B4**  (a) $\frac{3}{8}$  (b) $\frac{3}{8}$

**B5**  (a) $\frac{9}{100}$  (b) $\frac{9}{10}$  (c) $\frac{1}{100}$  (d) 0

**B6**  The girl is correct. Each ticket has the same chance of winning. The winning number is more likely to be a two-figure number because there are more of them but the boy has only one such ticket so the probability of a winning two-figure number being his is small.

## C  Throwing coins

**C1**  (a) $\frac{1}{4}$  (b) $\frac{1}{4}$

**C2**  (a)

| A | B | C |
|---|---|---|
| H | H | H |
| H | H | T |
| H | T | H |
| H | T | T |
| T | H | H |
| T | H | T |
| T | T | H |
| T | T | T |

(b) 3  (c) $\frac{3}{8}$  (d) $\frac{3}{8}$  (e) (i) $\frac{1}{8}$ (ii) $\frac{1}{8}$

**C3**  (a)

| H H H H | T H H H |
|---------|---------|
| H H H T | T H H T |
| H H T H | T H T H |
| H H T T | T H T T |
| H T H H | T T H H |
| H T H T | T T H T |
| H T T H | T T T H |
| H T T T | T T T T |

(b) (i) $\frac{1}{16}$ (ii) $\frac{1}{4}$ (iii) $\frac{3}{8}$ (iv) $\frac{1}{4}$ (v) $\frac{1}{16}$

**C4**  (a) 32  (b) 1  (c) $\frac{1}{32}$  (d) $\frac{1}{128}$

## D  Throwing two dice

**D1**  (a)

| A B | A B | A B | A B | A B | A B |
|-----|-----|-----|-----|-----|-----|
| 1 1 | 2 1 | 3 1 | 4 1 | 5 1 | 6 1 |
| 1 2 | 2 2 | 3 2 | 4 2 | 5 2 | 6 2 |
| 1 3 | 2 3 | 3 3 | 4 3 | 5 3 | 6 3 |
| 1 4 | 2 4 | 3 4 | 4 4 | 5 4 | 6 4 |
| 1 5 | 2 5 | 3 5 | 4 5 | 5 5 | 6 5 |
| 1 6 | 2 6 | 3 6 | 4 6 | 5 6 | 6 6 |

(b) 36  (c) 4  (d) $\frac{4}{36} = \frac{1}{9}$  (e) 3
(f) $\frac{1}{12}$  (g) Score of 7, $\frac{1}{6}$

**D2**  (a)

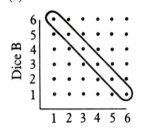

(b) $\frac{1}{6}$

**D3**  (a) (5, 4), (6, 3) and (3, 6)
(b) $\frac{4}{36} = \frac{1}{9}$

**D4**

| Total score with 2 dice | 2 | 3 | 4 | 5 | 6 | 7 | 8 | 9 | 10 | 11 | 12 |
|---|---|---|---|---|---|---|---|---|---|---|---|
| Probability | $\frac{1}{36}$ | $\frac{2}{36}$ | $\frac{3}{36}$ | $\frac{4}{36}$ | $\frac{5}{36}$ | $\frac{6}{36}$ | $\frac{5}{36}$ | $\frac{4}{36}$ | $\frac{3}{36}$ | $\frac{2}{36}$ | $\frac{1}{36}$ |

**D5**  (a) 6  (b) $\frac{1}{6}$
(c) $\frac{3}{36} + \frac{2}{36} + \frac{1}{36} = \frac{6}{36} = \frac{1}{6}$

**D6**  (a)

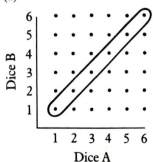

(b) $\frac{1}{6}$

**D7** (a)

Dice B axis: 6, 5, 4, 3, 2, 1
```
6 | .5 .4 .3 .2 .1 .0
5 | .4 .3 .2 .1 .0 .1
4 | .3 .2 .1 .0 .1 .2
3 | .2 .1 .0 .1 .2 .3
2 | .1 .0 .1 .2 .3 .4
1 | .0 .1 .2 .3 .4 .5
  +---------------------
    1  2  3  4  5  6
         Dice A
```

(b) 8

(c) $\frac{8}{36} = \frac{2}{9}$

(d)

| Difference between scores on two dice | 0 | 1 | 2 | 3 | 4 | 5 |
|---|---|---|---|---|---|---|
| Probability | $\frac{6}{36}$ | $\frac{10}{36}$ | $\frac{8}{36}$ | $\frac{6}{36}$ | $\frac{4}{36}$ | $\frac{2}{36}$ |

**E  Miscellaneous questions**

**E1** (a)
```
I   II  III
I   III II
II  I   III
II  III I
III I   II
III II  I
```
(b) $\frac{1}{6}$

(c) $\frac{1}{3}$

**E2** (a) $\frac{6}{24} = \frac{1}{4}$

(b) $\frac{6}{24} = \frac{1}{4}$

(c) $\frac{1}{2}$  (d) $\frac{1}{24}$

(e) $\frac{1}{12}$

**E3** (a) $\frac{1}{2}$  (b) $\frac{1}{2}$  (c) $\frac{1}{3}$

---

# 21   The circle

Section A reviews work on the circumference of a circle and introduces the formula $C = 2\pi r$. The rest of the chapter is concerned with the area of a circle and with the volume of a cylinder.

**A  The circumference of a circle**

**A1** (a) 12·6cm  (b) 17·3cm  (c) 33·9cm

**A2** (a) Divide the circumference by $\pi$.
(b) 23·7m (to 1 d.p.)

**A3** (a) 31·4  (b) 42·7  (c) 199·2

**A4** (a) 2·6cm  (b) 6·7cm
(c) 6·1cm  (d) 1·7cm

**A5** 61·1cm (to 1 d.p.)

**A6** 15·9cm

**B  The area of a circle**

**B1** (a) 147  (b) 156  (c) The answer to (b)

**B2** (a) 15·2cm²  (b) 8·0cm²

**B3** (a) 11·3cm²  (b) 24·6cm²
(c) 109·4cm²  (d) 243·3cm²

**B4** (a) 2·3cm  (b) 16·6cm²

**B5**

| Diameter | Radius | Area |
|---|---|---|
| (a) 2·6cm | 1·3cm | 5·3cm² |
| (b) 1·6cm | 0·8cm | 2·0cm² |
| (c) 3·4cm | 1·7cm | 9·1cm² |

**B6** (a) 8·0cm²  (b) 4·5cm²  (c) 3·5cm²

**B7** (a) Many pupils will think that it is less.
(b) (i) 10·2cm²  (ii) 12·7cm²
(c) Depends on pupil's own answer to (a)

**C  Mixed questions on circumference and area**

**C1** (a) 42·7cm  (b) 145·3cm²

**C2** (a) 63·6m² (to 1 d.p.)  (b) 9m
(c) 28·3m (to 1 d.p.)

**C3** (a) 13·8cm  (b) 54·0cm  (c) 128·7cm²
(d) 359·7cm²  (e) 40·8cm (all to 1 d.p.)

**C4** 9·5cm and 6·7cm (both to 1 d.p.)

**C5** (a) 346·4cm²  (b) 277·3cm² left (both to 1 d.p.)

## D  The volume of a cylinder

All answers except D8 are given to 1 d.p. The accuracy actually justified can be brought out in discussion.

**D1** (a) $50.3\,cm^2$ (b) $1005.3\,cm^3$

**D2** (a) $912.3\,cm^3$ (b) $563.0\,cm^3$

**D3** (a) $4.2\,cm$ (b) $415.6\,cm^3$

**D4** $160.7\,cm^3$

**D5** (a) $14.2\,cm^3$ (b) $1.4\,cm^3$

**D6** $1.2\,cm^3$

**D7** $1.6\,cm^3$

**D8** $1080\,m^3$ (to nearest $10\,m^3$)

**D9** $12.7\,cm$

---

# 22  On paper (2)

See the note on chapter 13.

| | | | |
|---|---|---|---|
| 1 | 347 | 6 | £3·45 |
| 2 | £1·10 | 7 | 34 bottles |
| 3 | £10·75 | 8 | (a) 78p  (b) £2·75 |
| 4 | 216 photos | 9 | £94·50 |
| 5 | 487 miles | 10 | 135 pages |

---

# 23  Sampling

The work in this chapter is intended throughout as a class activity, with class discussion of the results obtained in each case. The text is also there to be discussed, and for the teacher to enlarge on. The chapter is not intended to be 'self-instructional'.

**Equipment**: In section B each pupil uses a dice. One dice between two pupils should be sufficient.

### Introduction
A common problem in statistics is how to obtain information about a large population on the basis of a small sample chosen from it. A large part of the theory of statistics is devoted to the question of how reliable such information is likely to be, given (1) what is known about the population already, (2) the size of the sample, and (3) the method by which the sample was chosen.

If we are dealing with samples chosen by **random selection**, then the theory of probability can be used to assess the reliability of the information obtained. However, the chapter is written for pupils who are not in a position to appreciate this theoretical approach. (For the teacher who is interested in the theoretical background there are brief notes on some of the theory on pages 45–46 of this guide.)

In the chapter, pupils are asked to take random samples of various sizes from a population, and to use these samples to estimate numerical measures of the whole population. The actual values of these measures are known and are contained in this guide. The activity of the pupils consists of

(1)  seeing how much variation there is in the estimates based on different samples of the same size;

(2)  seeing how this variation decreases as the size of the sample increases;

(3)  seeing how close the estimates are to the actual values being estimated, and what size of sample appears to be necessary to get reasonably reliable estimates.

It is not intended that pupils should get an 'answer' to the question of what size of sample is necessary, or even a 'rule of thumb' for answering the question. The size of sample depends on the accuracy sought and on the distribution of values within the population being sampled. What may surprise some pupils though is the degree of accuracy which one can get with even relatively small random samples (as, for example, in the activity of estimating a mean height, described in section E).

## A  Representative samples

Obviously the opening part of this section is likely to be of greater interest near to the time of an actual election.

The later part of the chapter deals with **random** samples, where every member of the population has an equal chance of being chosen to be in the sample. But random sampling is not the only method of choosing representative samples. Here are some other methods:

### (1)  Systematic sampling

If we want a 10% sample, we could go through the population picking every tenth individual. This would only yield a representative sample if the population is not arranged in any way which might introduce bias. For example, if married couples are listed in the order man, woman, then every tenth individual will be a woman and the sample will not be representative.

### (2)  Attribute sampling

Another way of selecting a sample systematically is to choose an attribute which is believed to be totally unrelated to the measurement we are trying to estimate, and to make the sample consist of all those who possess this attribute. For example, the sample could consist of all people born on the 15th of the month.
(An activity which uses this kind of sampling is described in section H of the chapter.)

### (3) Stratified sampling

The population is divided into sub-groups, for example into age-groups, and the proportion of the population in each sub-group is assumed to be known fairly accurately. The sample is chosen so as to reflect these proportions.

### (4) Quota sampling

This is a form of stratified sampling. The interviewers are asked to interview a definite number, or 'quota', of each sub-group, for example, so many men aged 25–40, so many women aged 41–60 etc. The interviewer carries on until all the quotas have been reached. The selection of each 'sub-sample' may be carried out by random or systematic sampling, but often the interviewer will just stop people in the street and ask questions.

## B Estimating the size of a population by sampling

**B1** In the first activity pupils can see roughly the relative 'sizes' of the items in the population (the numbers of trees in the squares), and are asked to select a representative sample. Most are likely to do it on the basis of 'choose a big one, a small one, a middle-sized one, …'

The number of trees in each square is as shown here.

The total number is **487**.

| | 1 | 2 | 3 | 4 | 5 | 6 |
|---|---|---|---|---|---|---|
| 6 | 11 | 12 | 10 | 10 | 14 | 14 |
| 5 | 13 | 18 | 13 | 11 | 16 | 12 |
| 4 | 18 | 25 | 9 | 11 | 14 | 12 |
| 3 | 15 | 9 | 16 | 11 | 10 | 13 |
| 2 | 17 | 11 | 19 | 11 | 16 | 10 |
| 1 | 12 | 18 | 15 | 17 | 9 | 15 |

Some pupils may be quite good at choosing a representative sample in this way (in the sense that they get good estimates). But they would find it much more difficult if

(a) the number of squares is very large,

(b) you do not know what is in each square before you choose your sample.

This latter is the situation in the activity in section C.

**B2**   It is hoped that the results will at least show that random sampling gives no worse a group of estimates than 'choosing your own sample'.

The reason for using random sampling is to eliminate conscious or unconscious bias in the choice of sample. A pupil may say, 'Why can't I just pick numbers of my own?' But it is well-known from numerous experiments that there is a tendency for people to avoid pairs of consecutive numbers, 'special' numbers like 1 or 100, etc.

Only if the sampling has been by random selection can the theory of probability be used to assess the reliability of the information obtained, but this argument is not likely to make much impact at this stage.

## C   Using random sequences

**C1**   This table shows the volume in m³ of each of the 100 trees. (For example, the volume of tree number 46 is found in row 4, column 6, and is $0.52\,\text{m}^3$.)

|   | Second digit of reference number | | | | | | | | | |
|---|------|------|------|------|------|------|------|------|------|------|
|   | 0 | 1 | 2 | 3 | 4 | 5 | 6 | 7 | 8 | 9 |
| 0 | 0·21 | 0·26 | 0·38 | 0·41 | 0·12 | 0·20 | 0·44 | 0·31 | 0·40 | 0·28 |
| 1 | 0·39 | 0·34 | 0·16 | 0·21 | 0·27 | 0·31 | 0·23 | 0·43 | 0·17 | 0·34 |
| 2 | 0·37 | 0·18 | 0·18 | 0·39 | 0·34 | 0·16 | 0·23 | 0·34 | 0·37 | 0·23 |
| 3 | 0·35 | 0·26 | 0·21 | 0·21 | 0·10 | 0·26 | 0·43 | 0·13 | 0·36 | 0·12 |
| 4 | 0·17 | 0·25 | 0·25 | 0·32 | 0·33 | 0·27 | 0·52 | 0·27 | 0·18 | 0·22 |
| 5 | 0·30 | 0·20 | 0·23 | 0·15 | 0·50 | 0·51 | 0·15 | 0·42 | 0·18 | 0·37 |
| 6 | 0·11 | 0·29 | 0·22 | 0·24 | 0·45 | 0·20 | 0·40 | 0·24 | 0·50 | 0·19 |
| 7 | 0·22 | 0·37 | 0·32 | 0·26 | 0·35 | 0·32 | 0·17 | 0·53 | 0·12 | 0·29 |
| 8 | 0·36 | 0·22 | 0·33 | 0·44 | 0·48 | 0·34 | 0·52 | 0·32 | 0·47 | 0·24 |
| 9 | 0·43 | 0·14 | 0·15 | 0·38 | 0·54 | 0·19 | 0·46 | 0·19 | 0·55 | 0·39 |

*First digit of reference number*

The total volume of all the trees is **29·80 m³**.

Mark the estimates and the actual total on a number line, as before.

## D    Sampling from a large population

This section is an introduction to the main part of the chapter devoted to sampling from the databases.

You may wish to organise pupils into pairs for the work which follows. In that case for 'member of the class', read 'pair'. If the class is a smallish one, it may be necessary for each pair to generate two samples. (Make sure that each partner in a pair takes a turn at all of the tasks.)

## E    Estimating a mean

**E2**    (d)  The actual mean height of the girls in database G is 162·7 cm.

**E5**    The actual means are:
(a)  Waist 66·4 cm                    (b)  Armspan 161·5 cm
(c)  Head circumference 55·3 cm       (d)  Weight 53·6 kg

## F    Estimating a median

**F1**    The actual median weight of the girls in database G is 53 kg.

**F2**    The actual medians are:
(a)  Height 162 cm    (b)  Armspan 160 cm
(c)  Waist 66 cm      (d)  Head circumference 55 cm

## G    Estimating a percentage

**G3**    The actual percentage of boys in database B who wear glasses is 16·3%.

**G4**    For the actual percentages, see the summary data on pages 36–38.

## H    Scatter diagrams

Pupils should be encouraged to be honest about what they observe in the results of their own sampling. They must not be made to feel that somehow their own scatter diagram is 'wrong' or 'not a good one' if it does not appear to show any relationship between height and shoe size. And they should not be trying to see evidence of a relationship in their own sample because they think it 'ought' to be there. (If you look hard enough for what you want to find you will eventually find it!)

It is an inevitable consequence of sampling that sometimes a sample may fail to show a relationship which does exist in the population as a whole, and sometimes a sample may appear to show a relationship which does not exist in the population as a whole.

## Summary data

The summary data below will be found useful by teachers who wish to make further use of the two databases.

### (a) *Summaries for each individual variable*

All entries in the tables in this section are *percentages* of the total number of boys or of the total number of girls.

*Left-handedness*

|  | Left-handed | Right-handed | |
|---|---|---|---|
| Girls | 11·3 | 88·7 | 100 |
| Boys | 13·9 | 86·1 | 100 |

*Wearing glasses*

|  | Yes | No | |
|---|---|---|---|
| Girls | 23·1 | 76·9 | 100 |
| Boys | 16·3 | 83·7 | 100 |

*Month of birth*

|  | J | F | M | A | M | J | J | A | S | O | N | D | |
|---|---|---|---|---|---|---|---|---|---|---|---|---|---|
| Girls | 9·2 | 7·7 | 7·7 | 7·2 | 6·7 | 9·7 | 5·6 | 7·7 | 9·2 | 10·3 | 8·7 | 10·3 | 100 |
| Boys | 10·0 | 9·1 | 11·0 | 8·1 | 9·6 | 8·1 | 7·2 | 7·7 | 5·3 | 7·2 | 9·1 | 7·7 | 100 |

*Swimming*

|  | Can swim | Cannot swim | |
|---|---|---|---|
| Girls | 93·8 | 6·2 | 100 |
| Boys | 93·8 | 6·2 | 100 |

*Tongue-rolling*

|  | Can roll tongue | Cannot roll tongue | |
|---|---|---|---|
| Girls | 72·8 | 27·2 | 100 |
| Boys | 78·0 | 22·0 | 100 |

*Shoe size*

|  | 1 | 2 | 3 | 3½ | 4 | 4½ | 5 | 5½ | 6 | 6½ | 7 |
|---|---|---|---|---|---|---|---|---|---|---|---|
| Girls | 0·5 | 0·5 | 4·1 | 3·6 | 9·7 | 8·2 | 19·5 | 10·8 | 22·1 | 8·2 | 8·7 |
| Boys |  |  | 0·5 |  |  |  | 3·3 | 1·0 | 7·7 | 3·8 | 16·3 |

|  | 7½ | 8 | 8½ | 9 | 9½ | 10 | 10½ | 11 | 11½ | 12 | |
|---|---|---|---|---|---|---|---|---|---|---|---|
| Girls | 0·5 | 3·1 | 0 | 0·5 |  |  |  |  |  |  | 100 |
| Boys | 3·3 | 23·9 | 5·7 | 14·4 | 3·8 | 12·4 | 0 | 1·9 | 1·4 | 0·5 | 100 |

Height in cm

| | 130–9 | 140–9 | 150–9 | 160–9 | 170–9 | 180–9 | 190–9 | |
|---|---|---|---|---|---|---|---|---|
| Girls | | 2·6 | 26·7 | 54·9 | 14·9 | 1·0 | | 100 |
| Boys | 0·5 | 1·0 | 11·5 | 37·8 | 38·3 | 9·6 | 1·4 | 100 |

Mean: Girls 162·7   Median: Girls 162   Standard deviation: Girls 6·75
Boys 169·1   Boys 169   Boys 8·67

Waist in cm

| | 40–9 | 50–9 | 60–9 | 70–9 | 80–9 | 90–9 | 100–9 | |
|---|---|---|---|---|---|---|---|---|
| Girls | | 12·8 | 59·5 | 25·1 | 2·1 | 0·5 | | 100 |
| Boys | 1·0 | 1·0 | 13·9 | 58·9 | 19·6 | 4·3 | 1·4 | 100 |

Mean: Girls 66·4   Median: Girls 66   Standard deviation: Girls 6·62
Boys 75·9   Boys 75   Boys 8·11

Armspan in cm

| | 120–9 | 130–9 | 140–9 | 150–9 | 160–9 | 170–9 | 180–9 | 190–9 | 200–9 | |
|---|---|---|---|---|---|---|---|---|---|---|
| Girls | | | 4·1 | 36·4 | 45·1 | 10·8 | 3·1 | 0·5 | | 100 |
| Boys | 0·5 | | 0·5 | 11·5 | 32·5 | 37·3 | 16·7 | 0·5 | 0·5 | 100 |

Mean: Girls 161·5   Median: Girls 160   Standard deviation: Girls 7·92
Boys 170·4   Boys 170   Boys 9·58

Handspan in cm

| | 13–15 | 16–18 | 19–21 | 22–24 | 25–27 | |
|---|---|---|---|---|---|---|
| Girls | 5·6 | 41·5 | 49·7 | 3·1 | | 100 |
| Boys | 0·5 | 9·1 | 52·6 | 34·9 | 2·9 | 100 |

Mean: Girls 18·5   Median: Girls 19   Standard deviation: Girls 1·79
Boys 20·9   Boys 21   Boys 1·93

Head circumference in cm

| | 45–9 | 50–4 | 55–9 | 60–4 | 65–9 | |
|---|---|---|---|---|---|---|
| Girls | 0·5 | 33·8 | 63·6 | 1·5 | 0·5 | 100 |
| Boys | 1·0 | 13·9 | 79·4 | 5·3 | 0·5 | 100 |

Mean: Girls 55·3   Median: Girls 55   Standard deviation: Girls 2·07
Boys 56·3   Boys 56   Boys 2·13

*Weight in kg*

|        | 20–9 | 30–9 | 40–9 | 50–9 | 60–9 | 70–9 | 80–9 | 90–9 |     |
|--------|------|------|------|------|------|------|------|------|-----|
| Girls  |      | 3·1  | 22·6 | 54·4 | 16·4 | 2·6  | 1·0  |      | 100 |
| Boys   | 1·0  |      | 19·6 | 42·6 | 25·4 | 8·1  | 2·4  | 1·0  | 100 |

Mean:  Girls 53·6    Median:  Girls 53    Standard deviation:  Girls 7·70
       Boys 57·3             Boys 56                           Boys 10·19

**(b)  *Two-way tables of selected pairs of variables***

In these tables most of the measurements have been grouped. The entries are the actual numbers in the population.

The correlation coefficients have been calculated from the original ungrouped data. (See note on page 45.)

*Height, shoe size*

**Girls**

Shoe size (rows) × Height (columns)

| Shoe size | 140–9 | 150–9 | 160–9 | 170–9 | 180–9 |
|-----------|-------|-------|-------|-------|-------|
| 9         |       |       | 1     |       |       |
| 8½        |       |       |       |       |       |
| 8         |       |       | 2     | 4     |       |
| 7½        |       |       |       | 1     |       |
| 7         |       |       | 8     | 8     | 1     |
| 6½        |       | 1     | 10    | 4     | 1     |
| 6         |       | 3     | 30    | 10    |       |
| 5½        |       | 2     | 17    | 2     |       |
| 5         |       | 17    | 21    |       |       |
| 4½        |       | 10    | 6     |       |       |
| 4         |       | 10    | 9     |       |       |
| 3½        | 2     | 4     | 1     |       |       |
| 3         | 1     | 5     | 2     |       |       |
| 2½        |       |       |       |       |       |
| 2         | 1     |       |       |       |       |
| 1½        |       |       |       |       |       |
| 1         | 1     |       |       |       |       |

Height

(Correlation coefficient: 0·66)

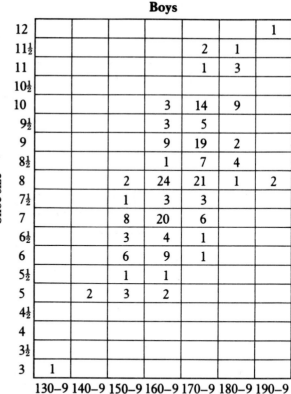

**Boys**

Shoe size (rows) × Height (columns)

| Shoe size | 130–9 | 140–9 | 150–9 | 160–9 | 170–9 | 180–9 | 190–9 |
|-----------|-------|-------|-------|-------|-------|-------|-------|
| 12        |       |       |       |       |       |       | 1     |
| 11½       |       |       |       |       | 2     | 1     |       |
| 11        |       |       |       |       | 1     | 3     |       |
| 10½       |       |       |       |       |       |       |       |
| 10        |       |       |       | 3     | 14    | 9     |       |
| 9½        |       |       |       | 3     | 5     |       |       |
| 9         |       |       |       | 9     | 19    | 2     |       |
| 8½        |       |       |       | 1     | 7     | 4     |       |
| 8         |       |       | 2     | 24    | 21    | 1     | 2     |
| 7½        |       |       | 1     | 3     | 3     |       |       |
| 7         |       |       | 8     | 20    | 6     |       |       |
| 6½        |       |       | 3     | 4     | 1     |       |       |
| 6         |       |       | 6     | 9     | 1     |       |       |
| 5½        |       |       | 1     | 1     |       |       |       |
| 5         |       | 2     | 3     | 2     |       |       |       |
| 4½        |       |       |       |       |       |       |       |
| 4         |       |       |       |       |       |       |       |
| 3½        |       |       |       |       |       |       |       |
| 3         | 1     |       |       |       |       |       |       |

Height

(Correlation coefficient: 0·53)

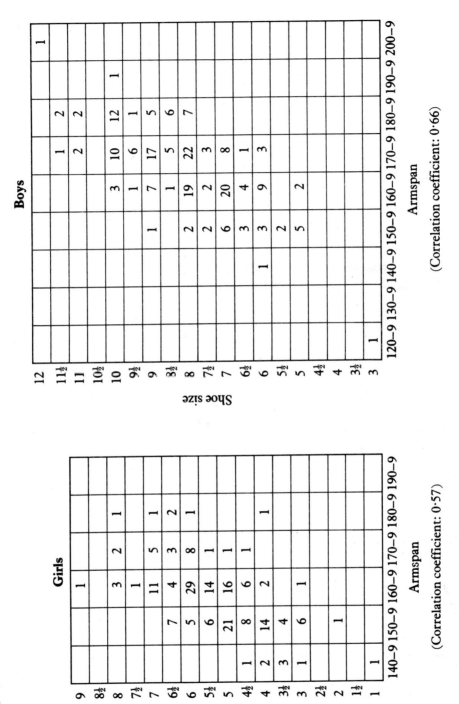

*Armspan, shoe size*

Girls

(Correlation coefficient: 0·57)

Boys

(Correlation coefficient: 0·66)

*Weight, shoe size*

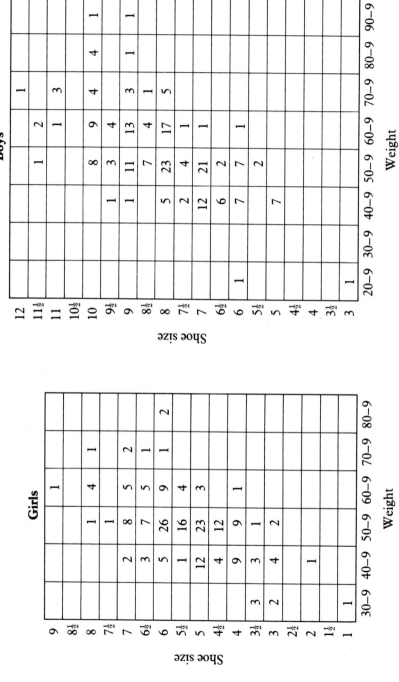

**Boys**

| Shoe size | 20–9 | 30–9 | 40–9 | 50–9 | 60–9 | 70–9 | 80–9 | 90–9 |
|---|---|---|---|---|---|---|---|---|
| 12 | | | | | | | | |
| 11½ | | | | 1 | 2 | 1 | | |
| 11 | | | | 1 | 1 | 3 | | |
| 10½ | | | | | | | | |
| 10 | | | | 8 | 9 | 4 | 4 | 1 |
| 9½ | | | 1 | 3 | 4 | | | |
| 9 | | | 1 | 11 | 13 | 3 | 1 | 1 |
| 8½ | | | | 7 | 4 | 1 | | |
| 8 | | | 5 | 23 | 17 | 5 | | |
| 7½ | | | 2 | 4 | 1 | | | |
| 7 | | | 12 | 21 | 1 | | | |
| 6½ | | | 6 | 2 | | | | |
| 6 | 1 | | 7 | 7 | 1 | | | |
| 5½ | | | 7 | 2 | | | | |
| 5 | | | 7 | | | | | |
| 4½ | | | | | | | | |
| 4 | | | | | | | | |
| 3½ | | | | | | | | |
| 3 | 1 | | | | | | | |

**Weight**

(Correlation coefficient: 0·62)

**Girls**

| Shoe size | 30–9 | 40–9 | 50–9 | 60–9 | 70–9 | 80–9 |
|---|---|---|---|---|---|---|
| 9 | | | | | | |
| 8½ | | | | | | |
| 8 | | | 1 | 4 | 1 | |
| 7½ | | | 1 | 5 | 2 | |
| 7 | | 2 | 8 | 5 | 1 | |
| 6½ | | 3 | 7 | 5 | 1 | |
| 6 | | 5 | 26 | 9 | | 2 |
| 5½ | | 1 | 16 | 4 | | |
| 5 | | 12 | 23 | 3 | | |
| 4½ | | 4 | 12 | | | |
| 4 | | 9 | 9 | 1 | | |
| 3½ | 3 | 3 | 1 | | | |
| 3 | 2 | 4 | 2 | | | |
| 2½ | | | | | | |
| 2 | | 1 | | | | |
| 1½ | | | | | | |
| 1 | 1 | | | | | |

**Weight**

(Correlation coefficient: 0·54)

*Handspan, shoe size*

**Girls**

| Shoe size | 13–15 | 16–18 | 19–21 | 22–24 |
|---|---|---|---|---|
| 9 | | | | |
| 8½ | | | 1 | |
| 8 | | 1 | 5 | |
| 7½ | | | 1 | |
| 7 | | 3 | 13 | 1 |
| 6½ | | 4 | 11 | 1 |
| 6 | 3 | 8 | 29 | 3 |
| 5½ | 1 | 7 | 13 | |
| 5 | 4 | 24 | 9 | |
| 4½ | 2 | 9 | 5 | |
| 4 | 1 | 11 | 7 | |
| 3½ | | 6 | 1 | |
| 3 | | 6 | 2 | |
| 2½ | | 1 | | |
| 2 | | | | |
| 1½ | | 1 | | |
| 1 | | | | |

Handspan

(Correlation coefficient: 0·37)

**Boys**

| Shoe size | 13–15 | 16–18 | 19–21 | 22–24 | 25–27 |
|---|---|---|---|---|---|
| 12 | | | | | 1 |
| 11½ | | | 2 | 1 | |
| 11 | | | 1 | 2 | 1 |
| 10½ | | | | | |
| 10 | | 8 | 8 | 16 | 2 |
| 9½ | | 1 | 1 | 6 | |
| 9 | | 1 | 11 | 18 | |
| 8½ | | | 5 | 6 | |
| 8 | | 6 | 32 | 12 | |
| 7½ | | | 6 | 1 | |
| 7 | 1 | 3 | 24 | 6 | |
| 6½ | | 1 | 7 | | |
| 6 | | 3 | 9 | 3 | |
| 5½ | | 1 | 1 | | |
| 5 | | 2 | 3 | 2 | |
| 4½ | | | | | |
| 4 | | | | | |
| 3½ | | | | | |
| 3 | | 1 | | | |

Handspan

(Correlation coefficient: 0·42)

*Height, armspan*

**Boys**

| Armspan \ Height | 130–9 | 140–9 | 150–9 | 160–9 | 170–9 | 180–9 | 190–9 |
|---|---|---|---|---|---|---|---|
| 200–9 | | | | | | | 1 |
| 190–9 | | | | | | 1 | |
| 180–9 | | | | | 15 | 2 | |
| 170–9 | | | | 17 | 52 | 4 | |
| 160–9 | | | 1 | 22 | 49 | 11 | |
| 150–9 | | 8 | 15 | 7 | | | |
| 140–9 | | 2 | 1 | | | | |
| 130–9 | | | | | | | |
| 120–9 | 1 | | | | | | |

Height

(Correlation coefficient: 0·52)

**Girls**

| Armspan \ Height | 140–9 | 150–9 | 160–9 | 170–9 | 180–9 |
|---|---|---|---|---|---|
| 190–9 | | | | | 2 |
| 180–9 | | | | 3 | 10 |
| 170–9 | | | 1 | 11 | 16 |
| 160–9 | | 6 | 66 | 29 | |
| 150–9 | 2 | 41 | | | |
| 140–9 | 3 | 5 | | | |

Height

(Correlation coefficient: 0·71)

*Height, waist*

**Boys**

| Waist \ Height | 130–9 | 140–9 | 150–9 | 160–9 | 170–9 | 180–9 | 190–9 |
|---|---|---|---|---|---|---|---|
| 100–9 | | | | | 2 | 1 | 3 |
| 90–9 | | | | 2 | 6 | 1 | 8 |
| 80–9 | | | 2 | 10 | 18 | 8 | 9 |
| 70–9 | | | 14 | 51 | 47 | 2 | |
| 60–9 | | | 6 | 13 | 8 | 2 | |
| 50–9 | | 1 | | 1 | | | |
| 40–9 | | 2 | | | | | |

Height

(Correlation coefficient: 0·19)

**Girls**

| Waist \ Height | 140–9 | 150–9 | 160–9 | 170–9 | 180–9 |
|---|---|---|---|---|---|
| 90–9 | | | | 1 | |
| 80–9 | | | 3 | 1 | |
| 70–9 | | 16 | 27 | 5 | |
| 60–9 | 4 | 29 | 65 | 17 | 1 |
| 50–9 | 1 | 7 | 11 | 6 | 1 |

Height

(Correlation coefficient: 0·01)

*Weight, armspan*

**Girls** — (Correlation coefficient: 0·41)

| Armspan | 30–9 | 40–9 | 50–9 | 60–9 | 70–9 | 80–9 |
|---|---|---|---|---|---|---|
| 190–9 | | | | | | |
| 180–9 | | | 1 | 2 | 2 | |
| 170–9 | | 2 | 10 | 9 | | |
| 160–9 | | 14 | 55 | 14 | 3 | 2 |
| 150–9 | 3 | 24 | 38 | 7 | | |
| 140–9 | 3 | 3 | 2 | | | |

Weight

**Boys** — (Correlation coefficient: 0·49)

| Armspan | 20–9 | 30–9 | 40–9 | 50–9 | 60–9 | 70–9 | 80–9 | 90–9 |
|---|---|---|---|---|---|---|---|---|
| 200–9 | | | | | | 1 | | |
| 190–9 | | | | | 1 | | | |
| 180–9 | | | 1 | 8 | 18 | 5 | 3 | |
| 170–9 | | | 5 | 37 | 23 | 9 | 2 | 1 |
| 160–9 | | | 20 | 36 | 10 | 2 | | |
| 150–9 | | | 14 | 8 | 1 | | | 1 |
| 140–9 | | | 1 | | | | | |
| 130–9 | | | | | | | | |
| 120–9 | 1 | | | | | | | |

Weight

*Weight, handspan*

**Girls** — (Correlation coefficient: 0·36)

| Handspan | 30–9 | 40–9 | 50–9 | 60–9 | 70–9 | 80–9 |
|---|---|---|---|---|---|---|
| 22–24 | | | | 1 | 3 | 1 |
| 19–21 | | 16 | 56 | 21 | 3 | 1 |
| 16–18 | 6 | 24 | 42 | 8 | 1 | |
| 13–15 | 4 | 7 | | | | |

Weight

**Boys** — (Correlation coefficient: 0·33)

| Handspan | 20–9 | 30–9 | 40–9 | 50–9 | 60–9 | 70–9 | 80–9 | 90–9 |
|---|---|---|---|---|---|---|---|---|
| 24–27 | | | | | 1 | 2 | 3 | |
| 22–24 | | | 5 | 34 | 21 | 6 | 5 | 2 |
| 19–21 | | 1 | 28 | 49 | 24 | 8 | | |
| 16–18 | | 1 | 8 | 5 | 5 | | | |
| 13–15 | | | | 1 | | | | |

Weight

**Boys**

| Weight \ Waist | 40–9 | 50–9 | 60–9 | 70–9 | 80–9 | 90–9 | 100–9 |
|---|---|---|---|---|---|---|---|
| 90–9 | | | | | | | 2 |
| 80–9 | | | | 1 | 2 | 2 | |
| 70–9 | | | | 2 | 8 | 6 | 1 |
| 60–9 | 2 | | 2 | 30 | 18 | 1 | |
| 50–9 | | 1 | 9 | 66 | 13 | | |
| 40–9 | | | 18 | 23 | | | |
| 30–9 | | | | 1 | | | |
| 20–9 | | 1 | | | | | |

(Correlation coefficient: 0·60)

*Waist, weight*

**Girls**

| Weight \ Waist | 50–9 | 60–9 | 70–9 | 80–9 | 90–9 |
|---|---|---|---|---|---|
| 80–9 | | | | | 1 |
| 70–9 | | | 1 | 2 | |
| 60–9 | | 1 | 2 | 2 | |
| 50–9 | 13 | 14 | 16 | | |
| 40–9 | 10 | 67 | 26 | | |
| 30–9 | 2 | 30 | 4 | | |

(Correlation coefficient: 0·49)

**Note on the correlation coefficients**

A correlation coefficient can (if positive, as in all cases here) be thought of as measuring the extent to which high values of one variable are associated with high values of the other and low values of one with low values of the other.

If the correlation coefficient has its maximum value of 1, then each variable is an increasing *linear* function of the other.

A negative correlation coefficient would indicate a tendency for high values of one variable to be associated with low values of the other, and vice versa. If the correlation coefficient is $^{-}1$, then one variable is a decreasing *linear* function of the other.

A correlation coefficient of 0 indicates the lack of any pattern of association between the two variables: high–high, high–low, low–high and low–low pairs all occur equally frequently.

## Notes on theoretical background

In statistics texts it is shown that if a random sample of size $n$ is taken from a large population whose mean is $\mu$ and standard deviation $\sigma$, then the mean value of the sample is distributed about a mean $\mu$ with standard deviation $\dfrac{\sigma}{\sqrt{n}}$.

What is confusing for many who first meet this statement in its theoretical form is the idea of a 'mean of means'. We have to imagine all the possible samples of size $n$ which can be drawn from the population. For each of these samples we can calculate the mean of that sample (by adding the values in the sample and dividing by $n$).

Some of these samples will be highly unrepresentative of the population as a whole, consisting of $n$ very large values or $n$ very small values, and in cases such as these the mean of the sample will be a long way from the mean of the population. In others, where the large and small values 'balance out', the sample means will be quite close to the population mean.

What we have, then, is a *distribution* of sample means. At one end of the distribution are the samples whose means are a lot less than the population mean. At the other end are those samples whose means are a lot more than the population mean. What the statement from the statistics textbook says is that distribution has the same mean value as that of the population itself, but there is less variation than there is in the population itself, the standard deviation being $\dfrac{1}{\sqrt{n}}$ of that of the population itself.

The graphs of the two distributions will look something like this:

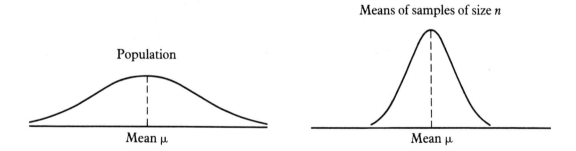

The shrinking of the amount of variation is due to the 'balancing out' effect, because there are a lot more possible samples in which large and small values 'balance out' than there are in which all the values are large or all small.

In some of the activities described in the chapter pupils in the class take different samples of a given size and look at the distribution of the sample means. They then observe how this distribution becomes less and less spread out as the sample size is increased. The degree of spreading is related to the reliability of the information obtained. As $n$ gets larger, the distribution of sample means becomes more heavily concentrated around $\mu$, and we can be more sure when we choose a sample that it will be one whose mean is close to $\mu$, the population mean.

Another activity described in the chapter is sampling to estimate the value of the percentage of items in the population which possess a certain attribute (for example, the percentage who wear glasses).

The standard result of theoretical statistics for this situation is as follows:

If a random sample of size $n$ is taken from a large population in which a proportion $p$ possesses a certain attribute, then the proportion of the sample which possesses the attribute is distributed about a mean $p$ with standard deviation $\sqrt{\left[\dfrac{p(1-p)}{n}\right]}$

The reason for the appearance of the word 'large' in the standard results quoted above is as follows.

Strictly speaking, the results apply only to (a) infinite populations; and (b) finite populations from which samples are chosen 'with replacement'. When a sample is chosen 'with replacement', the members of the sample are chosen one by one, each choice being from the *whole population*, so that it is possible for the same individual to be chosen more than once, and to be included in the same sample more than once.

The sampling in the chapter is sampling without replacement, because if the same reference number comes up twice in the course of selecting the sample, we have discarded the second occurrence and chosen a different number. However, if the sample size is small in comparison with the population size, so that the overall distribution of the population as a whole is not much affected by the process of taking out a sample, then the theoretical results are approximately true. Hence the term 'large'.

# Review 3

## 16  Simplifying expressions

**16.1**  (a) $2x + 4$  (b) $6 - 4x$  (c) $6 - 5a$
(d) $6 - 8b$

**16.2**  (a) 3  (b) 3

**16.3**  (a) $12ab$  (b) $12x^2$  (c) $35p^2q$
(d) $16bc^2$

## 18  Contours

**18.1**  (a) North side  (b) Left to right
(c) Downwards

## 19  Brackets

**19.1**  (a) $15a - 20$  (b) $18a + 6$
(c) $80 - 30b$  (d) $40 + 32x$

**19.2**  (a) 9  (b) 6·5  (c) 3  (d) $^-10$

**19.3**  (a) $ef - eg$  (b) $2ab + 6a$  (c) $3h^2 - 3hj$
(d) $4x^2 - 20xy$

**19.4**  (a) $6(x + y)$  (b) $5(a + 4b)$
(c) $4(3x - 4y)$  (d) $a(h + k)$
(e) $a(5 - b)$  (f) $n(3x + 4)$
(g) $3x(a + b)$  (h) $a(a - b)$

**★19.5**  (a) $x + 7$  (b) $x - 7$
(c) $x + 7 = 5(x - 7)$
(d) $x = 10·5$.  Each started with £10·50; then John had £17·50 and Janet £3·50, i.e. John had five times as much as Janet.

## 20  Probability

**20.1**  (a) $\frac{1}{6}$  (b) $\frac{1}{6}$  (c) $\frac{1}{12}$  (d) $\frac{1}{4}$  (e) $\frac{1}{4}$

**20.2**  (a), (b)

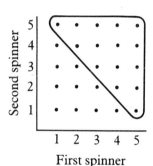

First spinner

(c) $\frac{15}{25} = 0·6$

## 21  The circle

**21.1**  53·4 cm

**21.2**  (a) $88·2\,\text{cm}^2$  (b) $54·1\,\text{cm}^2$

**21.3**  (a) $43·0\,\text{m}^2$ (to 1 d.p.)
(b) $1050\,\text{m}^2$ (to the nearest $10\,\text{m}^2$)

**21.4**  (a) $14·4\,\text{m}$ (to 1 d.p.)
(b) $163\,\text{m}^2$ (to the nearest $\text{m}^2$)

# M  Miscellaneous

**M1** (a)  Costs per m²:
A £4·76,  B £4·96,  C £4·39
So remnant B is the most expensive
material.

(b)  Remnant C   (c)  Remnants A, C

(d)

Using remnant A:

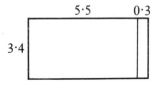

Using remnant C, five pieces are needed.
Two possible ways are:

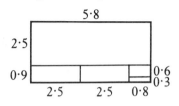

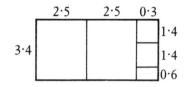

**M2**  670 m.p.h.

**M3** (a)  $4(4 + 2) = 24$  and  $5(5 + 2) = 35$
(b)  $w$ is between 4·5 and 4·6.
$w$ is 4·6 (to 1 d.p.).

**M4**  146 times per minute (to 3 s.f.)

Published by the Press Syndicate of the University of Cambridge
The Pitt Building, Trumpington Street, Cambridge CB2 1RP
32 East 57th Street, New York, NY 10022, USA
10 Stamford Road, Oakleigh, Melbourne 3166, Australia

© Cambridge University Press 1987

First published 1987

Typesetting and diagrams by Marlborough Design
Printed in Great Britain at the University Press, Cambridge

ISBN 0 521 31472 0